FAST AND FLUENT

Akhila Phadnis has done her Bachelors in Psychology from Women's Christian College (WCC), Chennai, and has recently completed her Masters in the same subject. She also has a Masters in Translation Studies and works as a professional translator. She enjoys reading, practising calligraphy (with Meghna), learning new languages and taking long walks by the beach.

Meghna Chandrika Narendran finished her Bachelors degree in Psychology from Ambedkar University Delhi and is currently pursuing a Masters degree in Social and Cultural Psychology at the London School of Economics (LSE). She has research and work experience in the related fields of anthropology, urban studies and literacy. She loves travelling and reading, dabbles in calligraphy, appreciates good television shows and is a compulsive list-maker.

FAST AND FLUENT
Memory hacks to learn any language

Akhila Phadnis
Meghna Chandrika Narendran

RUPA

Published by
Rupa Publications India Pvt. Ltd. 2019
7/16, Ansari Road, Daryaganj
New Delhi 110002

Sales centres:
Allahabad Bengaluru Chennai
Hyderabad Jaipur Kathmandu
Kolkata Mumbai

Copyright © Akhila Phadnis and Meghna Chandrika Narendran 2019

The views and opinions expressed in this book are the authors' own and the
facts are as reported by them, which have been verified to the extent possible,
and the publishers are not in any way liable for the same.

All rights reserved.
No part of this publication may be reproduced, transmitted,
or stored in a retrieval system, in any form or by any means, electronic,
mechanical, photocopying, recording or otherwise,
without the prior permission of the publisher.

ISBN: 978-93-5333-432-1

First impression 2019

10 9 8 7 6 5 4 3 2 1

Printed at HT Media Ltd, Gr. Noida

This book is sold subject to the condition that it shall not, by
way of trade or otherwise, be lent, resold, hired out, or otherwise circulated,
without the publisher's prior consent, in any form of binding or cover other
than that in which it is published.

Contents

Preface vii

Introduction xi

1. Memory: How It Works 1
2. Language and Learning 10
3. Using Memory and Techniques to Optimize It 22
4. Speaking and Listening 31
5. Reading and Writing 60
6. Techniques for Revision and Practice 85

Conclusion 112

Worksheets 117

Answer Key 147

Bibliography 149

Acknowledgements 152

Preface

'Memory' is a word that we all use very often these days. When looking at phones or laptops or other gadgets, people usually ask, 'How much memory does it come with?' And the answers range from 100 MB to 500 GB to 1 TB.

Now, imagine if we asked the same question about people: 'How much memory do we come with?'

The answer is—well, nobody knows!

Human beings have an amazing capacity to remember facts and events, and it seems as if nobody really knows how much we can hold in our memory.

Fans of the *Sherlock Holmes* series (books or the various TV adaptations) marvel at the detective's ability to easily recall names, faces and dates. But all of us have this capacity and use it without even realizing.

Think of how many lyrics you know by heart. Did you spend time memorizing them? Did you consciously make an effort to learn them? Everyone can recall facts and conversations from their favourite series—whether in books or movies. For example, some fans of the *Harry Potter* series can even recall page numbers of the books or entire conversations from their favourite parts.

Don't you quote your favourite dialogues from movies to friends? For example, if someone says, '*Don ko pakadna mushkil hi nahi...*' many Indians, even those who don't speak Hindi, will know the rest of the dialogue!

How are you able to do all this without even practising? You remember it simply because it made an impact. So, imagine, if you can do all of this without even so much as trying, how much more you would recall if you start noting things consciously and paying attention to them in new ways. It's time to train yourself to be Sherlock Holmes!

Here, we will start with a basic introduction to memory. What exactly is memory and where is it stored in our body? How does it work? We will see how information is stored in memory. We will then look at how languages are learnt—which is important, because it will tell you why some skills (such as speaking) may be easier than others (reading and writing).

Once you have a basic understanding of the way in which information is stored, we will then look at specific tricks and techniques to further explore how to efficiently store information and also how to select the relevant information.

The rest of the book will then help you adopt this knowledge and these techniques to learn languages better—whether it is to improve your vocabulary in languages you already speak or to enhance your ability to learn new languages. We hope the worksheets and exercises provided make this book an enjoyable read. See how easy it is to learn and apply these tips on a regular basis.

Finally, there is a summary at the end of the book and some blank spaces where you can note down your own techniques—things that you find helpful and which may not be mentioned here.

A tip: You don't have to read this book in any particular order. You can jump right into any section you like. You can even begin with the worksheets at the end of the book and refer to the techniques mentioned as and when you get to the corresponding exercises in the chapters!

This book is only meant to introduce you to certain techniques, but once you've got the basics, you can create your own methods.

Happy learning!

Introduction

Both the authors grew up in multilingual households. In Akhila's case, her parents speak two different Indian languages, Tamil and Marathi, which she learnt as a child, along with English. She grew up primarily speaking, reading and writing English and also learnt Hindi in school and French towards the end of her school life, while exploring other languages all along. She then continued with French through college and also later on.

While studying Psychology in college, Akhila was fascinated by the way people learnt things and how thinking occurs. Following this, she chose to work as a translator, which allows her to look at how people think *in* different languages and also how people think *about* different languages.

Meghna also grew up with English as the unifying language at home and it is now her first language. Travels, within and outside the country, led her to be exposed to new and varied tongues that she has tried picking up, albeit informally, in the past—from the Greek alphabet to Malayalam vocabulary to Czech orthography.

She also learnt Hindi and Tamil in school (but not very well, it turned out!). She briefly dabbled in Spanish, going for early-morning classes on weekends with her mother. She has many fond memories of them practising verbs in the car, studying for tests together and addressing each other by the

Spanish names assigned to them in class—Rosita Rojas and Sandra Gonzalez!

An important takeaway from this is that it's a great asset to have someone join in while you attempt to learn or improve your language skills.

Studying Psychology and Linguistics later in college helped Meghna understand the mechanism of learning and of languages, and also how to harness these. By breaking down sounds and words, and grammar and meanings, you really start to appreciate the phenomenon that is language, and both the authors hope that their love for languages comes through in this book.

Knowing multiple languages opens up new and exciting worlds, whether it is being able to manage in a foreign place, watching new films or making new friends. We become different people entirely, depending on the language we are using.

Our language-learning journey continues, slowly but steadily. We have personally used many of the tricks and techniques mentioned here in the recent past, in our travels and studies, and are happy to be able to share them with you.

Why this Book?

Many people think that learning a language is difficult and requires years of hard work. This is true to some extent. However, many people don't focus on the right techniques to remember words. Further, people often get scared by the different structures and sounds of a new language. We have seen people learning French or Spanish get discouraged because the sounds are too difficult or they can't understand how to form sentences. They also try and compare what they are learning with other languages they may already know—but they forget that, after all, people take years to become fluent even in their mother tongue.

The most important thing with any new language is accepting that it *is* new. That there are sounds you may never have heard before! How can you expect to learn them overnight? This is why we have included a chapter on how people learn languages (Chapter 2).

We hope that at the end of it, the readers feel like they can tackle any new language (or learn any subject, for that matter) and are able to modify techniques to suit themselves. One doesn't need to have the 'aptitude' for languages, or a particularly brilliant memory. All it takes is some patience, some work and a whole lot of excitement.

We hope to present to you a comprehensive picture of *effective* and *applicable* practices for learning, and improving your memory for language, dividing it among the four components: speaking, listening, reading and writing. Knowing that many Indians already speak multiple languages, we have used many examples from real life and worksheets to help you along the way.

Why Learn Languages at All?

While the brief introduction to the authors may have given you an idea of how they both took an interest in different languages, the reader may still wonder: 'Why is this important?'

After all, would it not be more useful to have books on how to improve memory with relation to Science or Maths? Why language then?

Here is why we think language is important and the reason we think that *you* should be interested in it too.

Language use is **social**. What this means is that you use language to communicate in a variety of situations. And based on this communication, events then unfold and people either do or say things in response. Language use is essential for humans. It greatly helped them develop, because information could now be passed on from one person to another and even between generations.

Imagine a scenario in your own life. A very simple thing: you want to tell your group of friends that you will join them in five minutes. How would you do this without language? Even gesturing would be impossible because the gestures for 'five', for instance, are only meaningful in languages that use numbers and have words or fixed gestures for them.

Similarly, how do you tell someone you're feeling upset or sad? How would you tell your friend about a great joke you just thought of?

Language helps people become social. You need language to communicate with other people, otherwise you will feel isolated. And this is one of the ways in which humanity has evolved and passed on information that helped the future generations.

Imagine warning people about dangers. If there was a quicksand in one place, an individual could warn his family or anyone who was nearby. But how would they tell others not to come there? Through language, the instruction could be passed around to the whole community or even other communities. And then, it could be passed on to the next generation so that children would not wander into it and when they grew up, they would tell *their* children, and so on.

Once writing was developed, it would become even easier. Someone could simply put up a sign saying 'DANGER: QUICKSAND' with pictures, too. The act of writing makes sure information remains and endures.

Think about this book. We are nowhere near you, but you are taking in and understanding every sentence we thought of.

Language is, therefore, essential in enabling communication.

Fluency in even one language means that you can communicate with people in that language and can also adapt what you say to different audiences. This is not possible unless you know synonyms for words, different ways of phrasing thoughts and also how appropriate these variations are for various contexts. You may not realize it, but you even think in a particular language.

For example, take into consideration how people adapt the kind of language (or **register**) they use in different contexts. The words you use when discussing an idea with a friend may not be appropriate to present the same in a meeting.

Here's an example: 'Whoa! So I have this utterly cool idea for a kickass phone! You can just blink at it and it will make calls and stuff! You just put in motion sensors!'

How would you pitch this to a professor or in a business meeting?

Perhaps something like this: 'My idea for a breakthrough innovation in cell phone technology involves motion sensors that can help the phone decode patterns in blinking to make calls, send emails, mute notifications, and so on.'

There's quite a drastic difference between the two, isn't it?

Further (and most importantly), fluency in a language makes it possible for you to enjoy different things: books, comics, jokes, music and, of course, TV shows and movies.

All these benefits only increase with the number of languages you speak. And different languages also help you see the world differently.

We chose this topic because we believe that language is

something people take for granted, without fully appreciating its role and value in our everyday life.

Hopefully, the strategies mentioned in this book can help you gain fluency in various languages and acquire new skills, both for pleasure as well as for professional and academic growth.

ONE

Memory: How It Works

To begin with, we are going to take a brief look at how memory is organized and how it works. There are several theories about memory and how it is structured. Most experts agree that there are two basic components of memory: storage and retrieval. What we usually mean by memory is that it is a stored collection of facts, figures, events, etc.; of course, the most important feature being that we are able to summon these up and 'remember' them whenever needed.

But let's be clear about one thing: memory is not a physical structure. There are different parts of our brain that play an important role in memory. But we can't point to a precise area and say '*that* is memory' and look inside it for stored images or videos, as we do on a phone or a computer. What researchers *have* been able to do is identify the primary structures associated with memory creation and storage. The most important of these is the hippocampus region.

We are so used to technology today that we imagine the human brain to be like a machine. However, you'd be surprised at how much more efficient your brain can sometimes be and how many connections it forms between hundreds and thousands of neurons—connections that get stored as memories.

Out of the various theories on memory, we will focus on

two of the most widely accepted ones: the **Modal theory** and the **Levels of Processing theory**. Both these theories explain several different aspects of how memory works and we will use them to help make learning more efficient.

> Let us look at a few basic terms:
>
> **Storage** or **encoding** is the term used for how information gets recorded in our memory.
>
> **Recall** is the act of finding and 'remembering' information that was stored earlier.

The Modal Model

This theory divides memory into three parts. When you first pay attention to something with your senses (touch, smell, sight, taste), it briefly registers in your mind and forms a **sensory memory**. If you then focus on this for longer, it enters your **short-term memory**, where it lasts for several seconds (like when you're looking up a phone number). However, if you decide you have no further use of this information, it fades away.

If, on the other hand, your mind forms connections and it is stored in your memory to be retrieved later, this information is said to have entered your **long-term memory**. If you don't use this information frequently, it becomes weaker and harder to remember.

Let's look at this in a little more detail. Think about the hundreds and thousands of things you come across in a day. If you're walking down a street, there are birds calling, people talking around you, cars moving, different objects on the pavements, on the roads... There are too many images, sounds, smells and sensations for your brain to be able to focus on at once.

Try this for yourself. Right now, look around you. Try and examine everything happening around you—the noises, the smells, the colours, the temperature, etc. The more you focus, the more you will realize how many things are happening simultaneously around you.

Is it easy? And, moreover, do you think you could handle so much information coming in every single minute of the day? It would be quite overwhelming.

So, what your brain does to avoid getting overwhelmed is to focus on a few specific things. If you're crossing the road, you tend to drown out the chatter around you, you ignore the hoardings or what people are selling—instead, you focus on the road and the traffic.

Similarly, if you're talking to your friend in a crowded area, you have the ability to focus on *only* what he/she is saying, even though about a hundred other people are talking around you. How does your brain do this?

This is done through a process called **selective attention**, where your brain quickly scans the environment, tries to identify what is most important or relevant and then 'focuses' on it, ignoring everything else. To be slightly poetic about it: it tries to find 'meaning' in the chaos around us.

When you do this, your sensory memory is activated. You become aware of something (it could be a sight, sound, smell, touch or taste) and your brain then interprets the information. If your brain decides to focus further on it, this event then enters your short-term memory.

Short-term memory is like a waiting area. Your brain takes in a certain amount of information. It gets stored in the short-term memory for a few seconds. If you decide to do nothing further with that information, it then gets erased and you don't 'remember' it.

It's as simple as that.

Let's take the example of a phone number. You need to call a shop to order groceries. You go online and look for their number. Say it's 2224445. You keep that number in mind as you dial it.

Then, when the other person picks up, you start talking. You don't need the number any longer and you are likely to forget it.

So here, your short-term memory helped you remember the information just as long as you needed to use it.

However, what if you keep dialling that number every day? Perhaps this shop sells your favourite chocolates and you order one every day. In that case, you will keep dialling that number and your brain will recognize that it is important. After a certain point, you will have repeated this number so often that it will be stored in your long-term memory.

There are many numbers we know by heart. Our parents' phone numbers, our best friends' numbers, our favourite restaurant's maybe…all of these are picked up because of a repeated action and the brain recognizing that it is significant information. This repetition is called **rehearsal**, and this is how information is stored and strengthened, according to this theory.

Of course, today, cell phones make all this much easier by storing names with the corresponding numbers. But it also means that you know fewer numbers 'by heart' and if your phone is not with you, you could be seriously inconvenienced.

Let us use another analogy for short-term and long-term memory. Imagine you're at school. You don't have paper. Your teacher assigns you some homework. You quickly grab a pen and write down the page numbers on your hand.

Now, there are two possibilities: you carefully copy this

information from your hand into your notebook; or, you go home, wash your hands and the information disappears. The first case is what happens in long-term memory. Information is transferred and carefully stored. The second case is that of short-term memory—you needed something and then it's gone without being more permanently stored.

In the context of learning a new subject, the first time you learn something, it gets stored in the short-term memory. Unless you revise it, your brain will soon begin to forget. However, if you go over the information, or if you share it with a friend, or if you see a film based on it, the information will become strongly recorded, over time, in your long-term memory, until it becomes a permanent feature.

Think of the time your parents bored you with facts they learnt in school. They might not be able to remember everything. However, the facts that they *do* remember are probably things they've studied over and over and over, until their brain refused to erase it.

Earlier, people used to assume that the only way to learn something new was to repeat it until you had it by heart (i.e. keep repeating it until it entered the long-term memory).

However, now that we know more about how memory works, we can use a combination of different techniques to ensure that the information from the short-term memory is successfully transferred to the long-term memory.

And this is where the Levels of Processing theory enters the picture.

Levels of Processing Model

This theory states that how deeply information is stored in your memory depends on how much meaning it has when you take it in. It says that instead of focussing on information being stored in sensory, short-term and long-term memory, what is important is *how* the information is learnt and what **meaning** it holds.

It talks about two ways in which information can be **processed** and is most applicable in the field of language and learning:

(i) **Shallow Processing**: This is information that is stored only superficially. This is either through **structural processing** (when only the physical appearance or major characteristics of something is stored) or through **phonemic processing** (when we register only the basic sound of something).

When you pass by a building and notice its shape or appearance, you are **structurally processing** the information. If you are listening to someone but not really paying attention to what they're saying, you could be said to be carrying out **phonemic processing**,

However, as the word 'shallow' indicates, both these are temporary memories and will soon fade away because there is no real meaning attached to the information.

(ii) **Deep Processing**: This involves **semantic processing**. It basically means that whatever new information or words you are learning are associated with earlier information you stored, so that it acquires proper meaning. This also explains why we may forget. You might find this true, even at school: any subject that interests you and that you go home and explore for yourself stays with you.

Although the two theories are different, they

offer exciting strategies for learning and optimizing memory. So, we will take the best from both theories in this book.

We will look at how you can improve your **attention** and **storage** techniques and derive the maximum **information** when learning something new. How well you remember something depends on how strong the memory is (how much meaning it has), and how long it has been since storage. Thus, proper storage will ensure easy recall.

Stress, Sleep and Memory

Research shows that **stress** affects both cognitive ability and memory processes.[1] Stress can be caused by several things: perhaps there is too much work, maybe you quarrelled with someone, or you have exams coming up. Either way, it is important to learn to cope with stress effectively. Try talking to someone or journaling. Pursue hobbies such as music or sports (this is exactly why they are called stress busters). Focus on your breathing.

Chronic stress (continuous stress) can even cause memory loss—that is, it doesn't just affect your ability to form new memories but erases existing ones as well.

Stress can, in turn, affect your **sleep**. Irregular or insufficient sleep affects **memory consolidation**. This means your brain's ability to correctly encode and store information decreases. The better you sleep, the better information

---

[1] Schwabe, L., Wolf, O.T. and Oitzl, M.S., 'Memory Formation under Stress: Quantity and Quality', *Neuroscience & Biobehavioral Reviews*, 34(4): 584–91, 2010.

> will be stored in your long-term memory. You may think that staying up late is cool, or cramming before an exam is helping but it is not. You need a good night's rest for information to be stored properly.

Forgetting

While we will look at the concept of forgetting closely in Chapter 6, the important thing to register is that forgetting is a natural part of our memory. It is inevitable. Many things you encounter will eventually be forgotten. This is simply because there is no need for it and, therefore, you do not **rehearse** the information. So, while forgetting is natural, what you need to ensure is that you actively keep reinforcing information valuable to you.

Worksheet

Let us revise what we have learnt so far. In the Modal theory, memory is assumed to have three structures or stages: sensory memory, short-term memory and long-term memory.

1. Can you match the right information to each structure/stage?

a)	Sensory memory	i)	Theoretically unlimited memory storage; information is stored here from a few minutes to a lifetime.
b)	Short-term memory	ii)	Impressions from the world around you when your brain uses selective attention to focus on some information, such as sight, sound, smell, taste, etc.

| c) Long-term memory | iii) A sort of waiting room for information. Information can last between fifteen to thirty seconds. About seven items can be easily stored at a time. |

2. Which of the following is true or false?
   a) We store information best when we attach meaning to it. (True/False)
   b) Any new number you dial is likely to be easier to remember than your best friend's number. (True/False)

TWO

Language and Learning

First and Second Languages

To begin with, let us first briefly look at how our brain learns language. Once you know this, you will be able to make more sense of what we suggest in the later chapters and can also modify these techniques for yourself.

The first thing to note is that there is a difference in the way you acquire a first language (L1) and how you go about learning second or third languages (L2 and L3). A first language is, quite literally, the very first language you pick up as a child from your parents/family. This could be one language or, if your parents or people around you speak different languages and, as a child, you pick them up around the same time, then it could be more.

The first language is **acquired** naturally because there is no conscious learning process involved. Even in the womb, you became aware of the predominant language spoken by your parents/family. When you are born, you can actually recognize voices or sounds you may have heard when you were in the womb. Now, as you grow up, in the first few months, you pay attention to the sounds around you. Up until babies are a few months old, they have the ability to distinguish between all the sounds that humans are capable of making. The more they are exposed to one or a few languages, the more they get used to them.

This indicates that memory is at work. Your brain is storing information on the language spoken around you and it helps you recall how this should sound. Your mouth and tongue then try and reproduce these sounds over and over (with encouragement and correction from adults) till you are able to pronounce the words correctly. At this point, your brain stores the correct pronunciation in your memory so you can use it every time henceforth.

Your mouth and tongue also remember how to use these sounds through something called **muscle memory**.

What is muscle memory?

In several chapters here, we will be talking about muscle memory. This refers specifically to a very special ability we have to learn skills through practice, until they become automatic. Muscle memory comes into play in any activity where the use of muscles is involved: dancing, writing, typing, playing a musical instrument, riding a bicycle, tying your shoelaces, etc.

If you think about it, for any movement, your brain needs to send a signal to different muscles. Some muscles have to extend; others contract. Just imagine what happens when you stand up; different parts of your body need to act independently.

Try it right now. Focus on your muscles as you stand up from a sitting position. Which muscles tighten? Can you feel them? What position are you in just before you raise your body? Are you placing weight on your arms? Now, try getting up from a different chair—one without arms. What happens now?

As you can see, your body remembers the different muscles needed for this action and sends appropriate signals to them. You can get up without thinking at all. For instance, you could be sitting and hear someone yelling for you. You jump up immediately and head over to them. You don't stop to think, 'Okay! First, I lean forward. Then, I put my weight on the feet. Then, I grip the chair.' If you did this every time you got up, you'd be wasting a lot of energy thinking about a very common activity and you'd take ages to perform it. Thankfully, it's a common and routine action. However, you didn't always *know* how to do this.

Have you seen those funny videos on the Internet of babies trying to sit up, get up or walk? It's quite amusing to see them get into various postures, make it to an upright position and then promptly totter over and sit back down with a bump. But toddlers practise this over and over again, until they can stand up or even take a few steps. Each time they do this, they are training their bodies to activate certain muscles. They are also strengthening these muscles. But even after strengthening them, the muscles require practice to learn the movements.

For example, if you have learnt swimming but let several months or years go by without doing it, the first time you get back to the water leaves your body feeling stiff and sore. And you will most probably feel clumsy and have some difficulty moving smoothly through the strokes. This is because while the memories are being revived (to put it simplistically), your body still needs some time to recall

> how exactly to coordinate the muscles and in what sequence to activate them.
>
> So, muscle memory is how your body remembers to carry out certain actions. These muscle memories are essential to human activities. Think about the most common activities you carry out without even thinking about it: walking, running, picking up spoons or bottles, cycling or even typing on your phone or keyboard. However, as with any other aspect of memory and learning, these activities must be practised. With long gaps in between, you may face some initial difficulty when returning to any skill.
>
> Can you guess where we'll be using this concept in this book? How about writing? How to hold a pen, at what angle to place your wrist, how to form letters—all these are skills our body learns. Similarly, when you speak, muscle memory helps you form sounds automatically, twisting or manipulating your mouth into different shapes.

You then go on to learn more vocabulary from other sources: people around you, books, movies, songs, etc.

However, as you would have noticed, you started the process of acquiring vocabulary and language rules from your L1, without any conscious effort. Human brains seem to come prepared to acquire language and we can see this in how babies learn grammar, without anyone explaining the rules to them.

One of the best examples of this is that even children who are just learning to speak, will say: 'Cat go' or 'Baby want'. The words are being used in the right order, even if the baby doesn't have the vocabulary to be more specific or articulate. So, the basic understanding of how words are put together, how adjectives and verbs are used, etc. is acquired through observation and repetition but is not actually taught to the child. In fact, if someone asks you about the grammar of your first language, or why something is said in a particular way, you might not be able to explain it, but simply say, 'I just *know* it!'

In contrast to acquisition of the first language, a second language must be **learned**. A second language implies that you already speak some other language (which is, obviously, not the case with babies and first language). It also implies that you *know* you are learning a new language; you are putting a *conscious* effort into learning. You are likely to compare this with your first language. And you will make a conscious effort to learn the rules of this new language. This can be either a language you use in everyday life, another language used in your own country or a foreign language. Like many multicultural and multilingual countries, India has the advantage of offering children multiple first *and* second languages. Some may even speak two languages from when they were infants; this is **bilingualism**. **Multilingualism** is the ability to speak more than two languages fluently.

Now, as we have explained the difference between a first and a second language, you will be able to understand why the following chapters focus more on **learning and memory for second language**, and **memory for the first language**.

We will give you tips on how to learn new languages and also on how to improve your knowledge of languages you already speak. Just to ensure that you understand the difference between a first language and a second language, look at the following example:

Aditi goes to an English-medium school, where they also teach Hindi. Her mother is Kannadiga. Her father is Malayali.

Categorize the following into Aditi's likely first languages and second languages: English, Malayalam, Hindi and Kannada.

> **Note: Indian English and language evolution**
>
> You may have come across someone who has told you, 'Hey, that's not an actual word, that's only Indian English!' What does this mean? Does this mean you are wrong?
>
> English was brought to India by the British hundreds of years ago, and has been integrated into our culture. It is even an official language. Many words have been borrowed into local languages from English and vice versa. Did you know the words 'jungle', 'juggernaut', 'bungalow', 'catamaran', 'cash', 'shampoo' and 'bandana' all come from Indian languages? Even words such as 'aiyo', 'guru' and 'karma' are considered English words. Have you come across any other Indian words in English?
>
> Indians have also developed their own version of the language over the years. It has different sounds, influenced by local accents (you will go on to read more about pronunciation and accents in Chapter 4), and has also developed its own words and phrases, that may or may not mean something different elsewhere. Some typical examples are 'prepone', 'do the needful', 'cousin brother/sister', 'history-sheeter' and 'air-dash'.
>
> A person with an Indian accent, when speaking English, does not, therefore, mean he/she is unpolished or is less knowledgeable about the language. It simply says that your speech is influenced by other Indian languages, and the way people speak around you.
>
> Language change like this happens organically and over a long period of time. Many linguists (people who study

> language) argue that there is no one 'correct' version of a language. It changes and evolves on its own, and as long as it serves the purpose of communication—people agree on the meaning and understand what others are saying—it is acceptable. Internet language and slang are great examples of this. Words such as 'meme', 'troll', 'hashtag', 'lit' and 'basic' have taken on an entirely new meaning, driven by the use of technology.
>
> So, is it wrong? Usually not! Unless it is completely against the rules of grammar and syntax, or you cannot understand what the other person is saying, it is acceptable.

Language Acquisition and Age

Language acquisition can be described as the process by which people, especially children, pick up a language, naturally and easily, without conscious efforts at learning it.

A lot of research has shown that our brains seem ready to learn language.[2] Children are born with the ability to take in sounds and learn how to reproduce them, learn grammar and start talking. However, in order to do this, they have to be exposed to a language in their environment.

There also seems to be a specific time period within which children must be exposed to language. The theory that language learning in humans is biologically linked to age is known as the **Critical Period Hypothesis**. Studies on children who were locked away or did not have human interaction in their early years show that unless a child is exposed to language in the first eight years or so, he/she cannot acquire language

---

[2]Pinker, S., *The Language Instinct: How the Mind Creates Language*, Penguin, UK, 2003.

later, and can only learn a few limited words or phrases.[3]

However, language is more than just a spoken set of sounds. Studies have shown that babies with hearing impairment find it difficult to learn a spoken language and can often lose out on acquiring language if they are not provided with other means of expression such as **sign language** in the critical period that we mentioned.[4] However, if parents and people around communicate to babies in sign language, then even from six months on, they can **babble,** making gestures with their hands. This was demonstrated in the study on deaf babies with deaf parents who used sign language with them.[5] It is further proof that human beings are primed to **communicate** with each other, no matter what the circumstances and limitations.

Why is this information relevant here? Well, the fact is that all of us have gone through this period of language acquisition as babies. We don't even remember how we learned (though our families usually have plenty of embarrassing tales to tell others about that one word that we always mispronounced)

---

[3]Purves D., Augustine G.J., Fitzpatrick D., et al., (editors), 'The Development of Language: A Critical Period in Humans', *Neuroscience*, 2nd edition, Sinauer Associates, Sunderland (MA), 2001. Available at https://www.ncbi.nlm.nih.gov/books/NBK11007/ (accessed in 2018)

Trafton, Anne, 'Cognitive Scientists Define Critical Period for Learning Language', *MIT News*, 2018. Available at http://news.mit.edu/2018/cognitive-scientists-define-critical-period-learning-language-0501 (accessed in 2018)

[4]Humphries, Tom, Kushalnagar, Poorna, Mathur, Gaurav, Napoli, Donna Jo, Padden, Carol, Rathmann, Christian and Smith, Scott, 'Avoiding Linguistic Neglect of Deaf Children', *Social Service Review*, 90(4): 589–619, 2016.

[5]*BBC News*, 'Hearing Babies Babble with Hands', 2004. Available at http://news.bbc.co.uk/2/hi/health/3894007.stm (accessed in 2018)

Leutwyler, K., 'Hearing Babies of Deaf Parents "Babble" with their Hands', 2001. Available at https://www.scientificamerican.com/article/hearing-babies-of-deaf-pa/(accessed in 2018) and always *just* remember being able to use our first language.

This discourages a lot of people when they're learning a second language. Research has shown again that children up to the age of ten can learn other languages without any accent. As research with babies has shown, very young babies can differentiate between various sounds.[6] For example, a baby may be able to tell the difference between the 'c' in 'cinema' and the more lisping sound used in the Spanish word 'ciento' (meaning, 'hundred') (pronounced more like *th* in 'thing'. Do look this up! Can you make out the sound?). However, quite early on, children start zooming in only on the languages they hear regularly and stop differentiating between other sounds. Thus, a child who speaks Hindi, say, where there is only one 'sa' sound (Saraswati, Dosa, Sumati, etc.) may no longer be able to differentiate between this sound and the Spanish one. We have given a more detailed example of this in the next part, so don't worry if this still appears a little confusing. The basic point is that once out of childhood, people find it harder to identify difference between new sounds they learn in a new language and in pronouncing them.

But contrary to popular perception, it is *completely* possible to learn new languages, even when you're sixty years old. It's just a slower process compared to say, an eight-year-old learning the same language. This can often discourage

---

[6]Trafton, Anne, 'Cognitive Scientists Define Critical Period for Learning Language', *MIT News*, 2018. Available at http://news.mit.edu/2018/cognitive-scientists-define-critical-period-learning-language-0501 (accessed in 2018)

Smith, D.G., 'At What Age Does Our Ability to Learn a New Language Like a Native Speaker Disappear?' *Scientific American*, 2018. Available at https://www.scientificamerican.com/article/at-what-age-does-our-ability-to-learn-a-new-language-like-a-native-speaker-disappear/ (accessed in 2018)

people and it makes them think that they're not *meant* to learn languages. Some people do find it easier to take in new linguistic information. However, as we have seen, every human being is meant to learn language. It's just a matter of learning them well and using your memory to store and recall facts correctly.

In fact, learning a new language as an adult is excellent for the health of your brain. Learning a new language is not only good for improving your memory and attention but is also known to slow down cognitive decline, or the ageing of your mind. It is excellent to improve your multitasking and decision-making skills, as well as your ability to perceive details in your surroundings. Studies show that bilingualism may even help slow down the onset of Alzheimer's disease in old age.[7]

Finally, let's talk about another difference between a second and a first language. When you learn a second language, you learn to speak, read and write around the same time.

However, in first-language acquisition, you acquire and can *understand* and *speak* your first language from childhood onwards because the brain is primed for speech. Nobody, however, simply acquires reading or writing. These skills need

---

[7] *Science Daily*, 'Bilingualism Could Offset Brain Changes in Alzheimer's', 2018. Available at https://www.sciencedaily.com/releases/2018/02/180206140713.htm (accessed in 2018)

Alzheimer's Society: United Against Dementia, 'Bilingual Brains are More Resilient to Dementia Cause by Alzheimer's Disease', 2017. Available at https://www.alzheimers.org.uk/news/2018-05-15/bilingual-brains-are-more-resilient-dementia-cause-alzheimers-disease (accessed in 2018)

Antoniou, Mark and Wright, Sarah. M, 'Uncovering the Mechanisms Responsible for Why Language Learning May Promote Healthy Cognitive Aging', *Frontiers in Psychology*, Vol. 8: 24–35, 2017. Available at https://www.frontiersin.org/articles/10.3389/fpsyg.2017.02217/full (accessed in 2018)

to be taught to you separately and, usually, are taught two years after you start speaking. I'm sure everyone remembers learning to read and having difficulties with certain spellings. Reading and writing are skills that need to be developed throughout our life. This is why, in the chapters that follow, we have broadly divided strategies into: speaking and listening, and reading and writing.

Worksheet

1. Draw up a list of the people you grew up with (parents, siblings, grandparents, etc.). Now, for each person, write down all the languages they speak, their mother tongue as well as any other language they may have learnt. Classify them as L1 (first language) and L2 (second language).

   _____
   _____
   _____
   _____

Now, write your own name and the names of all the languages you speak or are learning currently. Compare this list to your family's list.

_____
_____
_____
_____

Do you speak any languages that they don't? Do they speak languages you don't know? Which are your L1 and L2?

_____
_____
_____
_____

2. Have you ever thought about how *you* acquired your first language? Why don't you ask your parents or relatives some of these questions and find out? Write down your answers here.
   At what age did I start speaking?_____
   What was my first word? _____
   Did I speak any other languages? _____
   What were some of the funny words I used to say? _____
   Are there any words I found difficult? _____
3. For the next exercise, read this poem ('The Centipede's Dilemma' by George Humphrey[8]) out loud.

   A centipede was happy—quite!
   Until a toad in fun
   Said, 'Pray, which leg moves after which?'
   This raised her doubts to such a pitch,
   She fell exhausted in the ditch
   Not knowing how to run.

It talks about the simple processes our body performs every day that we take for granted, such as walking. The poor centipede in the poem forgot how to walk when he tried to focus on the movements of its legs. This relates to what we talked earlier regarding the role of muscle memory; how some movements become second nature to us. Can you think of any other activities you perform every day that involves the use of muscle memory and which actually become more complicated if you try and focus on each action that makes up that movement?

---

[8]Craster, K., 'The Centipede's Dilemma', *Pinafore Poems*, 1871.

THREE

Using Memory and Techniques to Optimize It

Now that we have looked at what memory is and how languages are learnt, let us review some basic techniques people use to store information.

Association

The most important concept that helps in storage and recall is **association**, an integral part of the theories of memory we are using.

Associations are connections that your brain makes between all the information it has stored. For example, if you hear the opening music to your favourite song, you immediately start singing the words. Why? Your brain makes the connection between that music and the words that follow.

Similarly, suppose you're at someone's house. A cake is brought out and candles are lit. Everyone suddenly starts singing 'Happy Birthday'. How do you know that you have to do this? Did you do this the first time you went for a birthday party? No. But the next time it happened, your brain noted the fact. So, the association between a cake with a message, candles, and people singing and clapping is very strong. This is probably something you will never forget in your life—

wherever you are, you'll join in and start singing along. And wherever you see a cake or a candle, you're likely to think of all the other things, even when they're not there.

Interestingly, the more associations you have with something, the stronger that memory is. When we say a memory is strong, we mean that you can easily recall it.

Let's look at how this can work in school: you learn about the concept of Matter in Physics ('Matter can neither be created nor destroyed', 'Matter can be solid, liquid, gas', etc.). This becomes a fact and your brain remembers it.

Then, you suddenly learn in Chemistry that Matter exists in three forms and you learn methods to convert it from liquid to gas or gas to liquid or liquid to solid.

Then, once you grasp the concept, you may learn in Geography class about the water cycle; how water in the atmosphere evaporates creating clouds, and then precipitates as rain or snow or even hail.

Because you already learnt about these three states, first in Physics, then in Chemistry, and then in Geography, your brain can make the connection much faster and you now have two or three associations with Matter, spanning different subjects. The more associations you have with a concept, the faster you are able to learn any related item.

This, of course, is how the education system is structured. You first learn simple Maths (numbers). Then, you learn how to do addition and subtraction, and then, multiplication and division. Then, you move on to fractions and algebra. Then, you explore trigonometry. You also start doing more sums in Physics, which involve the application of ideas you learnt in Maths…What you are doing is associating more information and strategies with what you already know. So, your entire school life is actually spent towards building associations and learning more by connecting anything you learn to previous information.

Think of a new fact as a boat. Your mind is the sea and there's a random fact floating on it, like a boat on water.

Let's go back to the example of Matter. When your brain forms an association—solid, liquid, gas—then that 'boat' (the word 'matter') gets tied down with one rope. When your brain starts forming more associations, more and more 'ropes' are tied around that word or concept, making it more stable. Suddenly, you have five or six ropes holding it firmly in place. The more ropes you add, the more firmly this boat is anchored.

Why is this relevant in this book? Well, if you're learning a new language, then the first couple of words will always be difficult to learn. It won't have too many associations and you'll need to put in a lot more effort into remembering them. But as you start learning more words and can form sentences, these words will start connecting to each other. You'll notice patterns in spellings, sounds and how they are arranged in a sentence. You'll suddenly find that instead of two or three words a day, you're learning seven or eight new sentences.

Repetition v/s Elaboration

Let us look at different ways in which associations can be built and recorded. Now that we have looked at so much information, let us try to understand why some things are easier to memorize than others.

Think of the number 0804328853.

Keep repeating this number to yourself. Do it thrice. Now close the book and try to recall the number. How many digits were you able to recall?

The problem with repeating random information is that

your brain doesn't really have anything to connect it to. These digits can't connect to any other memories you have, so it becomes harder to store it in your long-term memory.

Now, let us look at one simple fact. I know that 080 is the dialling code for Bengaluru.

Now, I'm sure if you try and repeat that number to yourself, you will remember at least the first three digits even a day or two later. This is because your brain immediately connected that information to other information that exists in your memory.

Exercise

Write down 080 on a paper. Now, given that you know it's the extension for Bengaluru, write down any information that comes to your mind when you think about what that number means.

Anything at all!

Here's a list one of us came up with in about forty seconds:

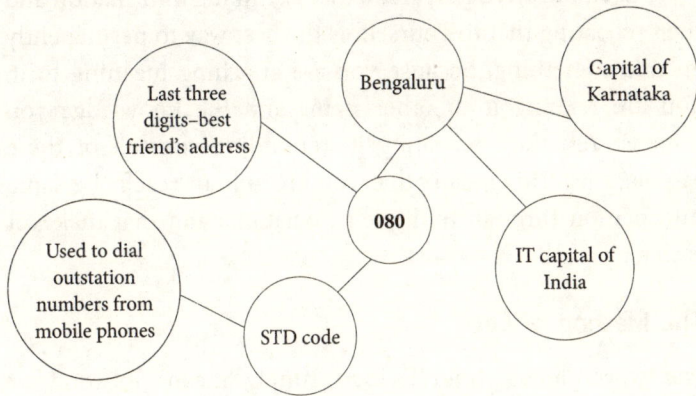

As you can see, in a few seconds, I've suddenly got so much information associated with 080.

The more associations you form, the stronger the memory. In this case, I have three direct associations (STD code, Bengaluru, last three digits of my best friend's address).

So now, every time I think of my best friend's address, I'm likely to think of the STD code for Bengaluru—080!

How about you? Time yourself. In one minute (or 1.5 minutes), write down 080-Bengaluru and everything that you think of that is associated with this. Don't hesitate. As you can see from my list, the associations can be as random as you wish. And each association that you jot down may lead to new connections that are not directly related to the original piece of information.

What we just did above—linking a piece of information to another we already know—is called **elaboration**.

Sometimes, you don't have an option. You need **repetition** to remember something, especially if it's the first time you're encountering such information.

But **elaborative rehearsal**, that is, linking information and then repeating that to yourself, is the best way to permanently encode something, because you are attaching meaning to it. You are relating it to other items and the knowledge you possess, and then repeating it, reminding yourself of these associations. This means that you are able to reach the same information through multiple associations and that makes it easier to recall.

The Method of Loci

The word 'locus' (plural: loci) simply means location or position. Therefore, the Method of Loci is one that involves imagining the positions of information to be remembered. It is actually a technique used to list out items.

Here's how it works. Imagine a path from your front door to your gate. Now, imagine that everything you need to remember is lying in specific places along that path. The logic is that if you associate things to remember, with places that are already very familiar to you, then the memory is more likely to be stored for longer periods of time.

For example: Here is your shopping list for today: tomato, onion, lemon and orange.

Now, think of your house. Imagine walking from the door of your house to the kitchen.

Look at the chair in the hall. Imagine a tomato there. Now look at your dining table. Imagine a lemon and an orange lying on the table, next to a bottle of water. Now, finally, imagine your kitchen and the sink there. Imagine an onion in the sink.

Think of this once again, with all the objects in the same places. Take a few seconds to close your eyes and make this image as vivid as possible.

When we use this technique in this book, we are going to adapt it a little and we are going to look at how you can easily learn some new basic vocabulary using your house or places that are familiar to you.

You can either do this in your imagination, or do this in real life, if you are in that location. We promise this will be a fun activity.

Now, without going back to the earlier paragraphs, can you recall the four objects that you were asked to place throughout your house?

Chunking

Though repetition is not a great way to remember things, sometimes, especially for new numbers or words, you need to keep repeating things in order to learn them.

However, rather than repeating endless facts (which gets very long and difficult), you could use chunking. In fact, we're sure many of you do this already.

Look at the below number and memorize it by repeating it about four to six times:

198745678910

Now, close the book and try and remember the number. Write it down. How much of it could you remember?

More importantly, *how* did you first repeat the numbers to yourself?

If you say '1-9-8-7-4-5-6-7-8-9-1-0', it's pretty certain that you remembered maybe four or five digits at most! But what most of you would have done instinctively was to **break up** the numbers into smaller groups.

For example: We broke it up in the following manner: 1-987-456-789-10. All we needed to do was two repetitions to remember this and write it, without looking at the number.

This breaking up of information into smaller parts is called **chunking**. Often, chunks of two or three units are most effective. We will be using this to learn how to break up new greetings and words in a new language.

Mnemonic

Technically, a mnemonic is anything that helps you store information and retrieve it. But in general use, it usually means shortcuts to remember information using acronyms, acrostics, etc.

An **acronym** is a word formed by using the first letter(s) of a set of words to make a shorter new word that reminds you of the original phrase or term. Often, these derived words become so common, we forget what they were supposed to stand for. For example, RADAR is **Ra**dio **D**etection and **R**anging and ATM is **A**utomated **T**eller **M**achine. Some other everyday examples of acronyms are scuba, laser, PIN and DVD. It is even commonly used in Internet slang: lol, btw, brb, rofl.

Acronyms can also be used while learning new words or terms. One of the most famous of these is VIBGYOR or ROY G VIB to teach us the colours of the rainbow. It doesn't really mean anything, but it gives all the clues you need to recall the colours and that too in the right order.

Another famous example of a mnenomic is the song 'Do(e) a Deer' from *The Sound of Music*. If you do not know this song, do ask someone to play it for you. In this song, Julie Andrews' character teaches children the Western musical notes (Do Re Mi Fa So La Ti Do) through a song, each note having a line of its own! 'Do(e) a deer, a female deer, Ray (Re), a drop of golden sun...' and so on.

There was a similar Hindi song ('Sare Ke Sare') used to teach the Indian classical music notes (Sa Re Ga Ma Pa Dha Ni Sa) from the film *Parichay*. Do listen to it as well.

How do mnemonics help in learning language? They may not be immediately useful, but they can help learning technical aspects of grammar or even for making lists of words.

Exercise

One of the mnemonics used to teach children the order of planets (from the sun) used to be:

My **V**ery **E**legant **M**other **J**ust **S**erved **U**s **N**ine **P**izzas.
= **M**ercury **V**enus **E**arth **M**ars **J**upiter **S**aturn **U**ranus **N**eptune **P**luto

However, Pluto is no longer a planet. So, can you and your friends make a new mnemonic?

We've given you a suggestion just to show you how it works.

My **V**iva **E**xamination **M**ay **J**ust **S**implify **U**nderwater **N**avigation.

As you can see, the sentence doesn't have to make much sense! It has to be vivid and easy to remember. Try and make up something as unique as possible.

FOUR
Speaking and Listening

Speaking and listening are the most instinctive elements of learning a language. This is how we learn languages as infants after all, without even trying! Babies pick up language by simply listening to sounds from the world around them and trying to mimic them. Often this results in amusing babbling and gibberish.

Sounds

If you flip through TV channels or travel to an unfamiliar place, you may find that the language spoken is not only different from the ones you can understand, but even the sounds may be unfamiliar. If you try to mimic these sounds, it is unlikely you will be able to pronounce them.

Humans are capable of producing up to a hundreds different sounds, known as **phonemes**. These sounds are produced using different parts and muscles in the mouth—your lips, your tongue, your teeth, the roof of your mouth, the back of your throat—and all this without even being conscious of it. Sounds can be full-throated yells, breathy whispers, or sometimes, even clicks.

Phonemes are the basic building blocks of words. Just imagine, the combinations of these few basic sounds are used to make thousands and thousands of words and languages, across the world.

As babies, all sounds were new to us, but we had the ability to learn and distinguish between all of these. However, the more we were exposed to our mother tongue(s), the more we got attuned to the sounds of those languages and ended up blocking out other sounds.

Different languages make use of only limited sets of these sounds. For example, Rotokas, a language spoken on an island in Papua New Guinea, has only eleven phonemes. Imagine using only eleven different sounds while you are talking. In contrast, take Taa (or !Xóõ), spoken in parts of southern Africa, which has up to a 117 different sounds, including clicks.

In comparison, Standard English uses about forty-four unique sounds. (Yes, there are only twenty-six alphabets, but remember that they can take on different sounds and combinations. For example, 'C' is pronounced differently in 'spaces' and 'cat'.)

As we mentioned earlier, being exposed to only a limited range of sounds growing up, a native speaker of one language may not even be able to distinguish between sounds foreign to him/her. For example, if a Hindi speaker were to listen to a conversation in Tamil, he/she may not be able to distinguish between the two different 'la' sounds that Tamil has, or the 'zha' sound unique to some South Indian languages, let alone pronounce them. Similarly, if a Tamil speaker were to try and quote a favourite Urdu couplet, he/she may not be able to pronounce the 'kha', 'dha' or 'gha' sounds and, again, may not realize that they are different from the 'ka', 'da' or 'ga' sounds that appear in Tamil.

And it is not just sounds that differ; languages often have a tune (or **intonation**) of their own, and syllables may be stressed differently. For example, an Indian speaker of English, probably as a second or even third language, is likely to say the word 'develop' as 'DEV-lup' as opposed to the British or American pronunciation, 'de-VEH-lup'. **Accents** develop because the way your muscles are trained by your native tongue affects your pronunciation of new words and sounds. Most interestingly, a study by Dr Kathleen Wermke and her colleagues found that babies even cry with a distinctive accent, depending on their mother tongue.[9]

Some sounds may also take some extra effort. We may have to think about where to place our tongue and what shape our mouth takes. In these cases, it may help to watch people speak and try and focus on how they speak. But, with enough practice, it will start to come naturally to us. The mistake many learners make is to feel self-conscious and not try. This means that they will not give their mouth muscles enough training and so truly never learn.

Therefore, when learning a new language, it is important to try and be conscious of the sounds and how we pronounce them. Often, losing our accent is one of the hardest things to do, and can end up sounding quite odd and exaggerated. Again, this is a normal process of learning a new language and you must not let it put you off.

When listening, it is important to also recognize the different **accents** a language may be spoken in. Very simplistically, an accent is a characteristic way of pronouncing words and speaking. It can often spill over into other languages.

For example, in *The Pink Panther* movies, part of the

---

[9] Post Staff Report, 'Le waaah! Babies Cry in Accents', *New York Post*, 6 November, 2009. Available online at https://nypost.com/2009/11/06/le-waaah-babies-cry-in-accents (accessed in 2018)

humour is derived from the fact that Inspector Clouseau speaks English with a strong French accent.

An accent is not something that should be mocked, as it simply reflects the influence of the speaker's mother tongue. If a person speaks with an accent, it proves that he/she is multilingual.

Here are a few things we can do to learn new sounds better and also to improve our pronunciation.

Repetition

When you hear 'repetition', you probably instantly think of some teacher asking you to read or repeat a word or phrase, sometimes over and over. This is not only tiresome but often doesn't work. By repetition, we don't mean you should get a long list of words and then say or read it, over and over. This particular method may not be helpful because:

- You will find that you will soon forget what these words mean.
- You may even forget why you wanted to learn them in the first place.
- You may get confused between words on the list, and not be able to recall the appropriate ones.

If you recall what we said in the first chapter, memories are only stored when the brain recognizes the value/meaning of a piece of information. If everything appears new and confusing, it won't hold any value.

What we mean by repetition is that when learning new sounds in a language, the only way to master them is to try it out for yourself, paying close attention to what you're doing. Your mouth may feel strange initially and your tongue may feel like it is flopping about. This is because you may be using some muscles for the first time. This is a good thing—the more you use them, the more attuned your muscles and brain become. You are building **muscle memory**, as discussed earlier.

Repeat sounds out loud, and focus on how you are saying them. Also, notice where your tongue is and the shape of your mouth when you are articulating the sounds. The more you say it, the more you will start to notice subtle differences in the sounds.

One good way to evaluate how far you've come is to record yourself saying a word or sentence. Then practise it for a while, record it again and compare the two recordings. Even a few minutes of practice will make a difference.

If you need help to verify, ask someone—your teacher or a classmate. Or, just do the old-fashioned thing and pull out a dictionary; they often have pronunciation guides (phonetic transcriptions), and may even have pictures of what shape your mouth should take while pronouncing the sound. Maybe turn on a film and imitate the way the dialogues are spoken. Again, do not be discouraged if you don't easily get your mouth in the right shape. Some sounds are new to us. Other sounds, however, could be very easy, thanks to other languages we speak.

Let us take, for example, the Spanish sound 'rr'. Many English speakers find it hard to articulate it, but speakers of Indian languages may find it a bit easier. We have many 'r' sounds in our languages. The Rs in Spanish have to be rolled, thus making a trilling noise, in quite an exaggerated manner. If we were to try and learn it, we would repeat the sound out loud—rrrrrr (like an engine). Try and make it as exaggerated as possible. Try and make a funny expression. Open your mouth as wide as you can. This helps you train your muscles, as the exaggerated position is unusual. This way, it will remain longer in your memory.

As part of the exaggeration, try and consciously adopt the accent of whoever you are observing.

For example, if you are learning French, it helps to understand how they *see* letters.

A student learning French can look at the following text and try to read it aloud with a French accent: 'My name is Philip. I have an elephant and three horses.'

Now, the French language tends to stress the 'i' sounds, and 'A-N-T' in any word is pronounced 'aw' with a nasal touch.

So, if you pretended to be French, you could read that out as: 'My name ees Phileep. I 'ave an elay-fawn and zree "orses".'

Use this to read out any English text following French rules of pronunciation. If you're learning Bengali, try reading any words in your languages with the accent you hear Bengali speakers use. You can do this with several different languages and it will help you memorize how certain letter patterns are pronounced.

However, be careful to not let **interference** affect the way you normally speak English or any other language in ordinary settings. It might seem strange to your Telugu family, for instance, if you start speaking Telugu to them in a Bengali accent.

Association

Once you have learnt a new sound, you will still need to be careful when using it, making sure your mouth and tongue are in the right position. For example, when Meghna practises her Spanish, she tries to remember how to make the sound. She would think of the ticklish feeling in her mouth when she tries making the sound or thinks of the expression that she usually makes when she pronounces it.

You could also try and find other words using that sound. In the case of the Spanish 'rr', some words are 'pe**rr**o' (dog), 'a**rr**oz' (rice) and 'co**rr**er' (to run). Using the sound in context—that is, as part of a word, instead of just trying to say 'rrrr'—will help you understand how the phoneme is used, how better to pronounce it, and will later remind you how to say the sound the next time you come across a word with it.

When you use another word or a sensation to remind yourself of a new one, you are creating an **association**. The stronger the associations, the more likely you are to remember. This is why languages get easier as you learn more words—you have more information to form associations with.

Variety is key here. Repeating the same word can be boring and using more words makes sure that the sound is properly fixed in your head, regardless of the length of the word or surrounding letters. For example: to try and see if you can roll your Rs like the Spanish, you can use 'arroz' and 'perro', but these are easy and the 'rr' is in almost the same place. What about a more challenging word like 'abu**rr**ido' (bored) or 'greco**rr**omano' (Greco-Roman). As you can see, practising with just one kind of word does not mean you will always pronounce it correctly. The more variety you introduce, the stronger the muscle memory becomes.

Going pro: Learn the International Phonetic Alphabet (IPA)

If you're interested in the pronunciations of words, you might want to look up the International Phonetic Alphabet (IPA). The IPA is a script used just to denote pronunciations: the sounds (phonemes), as well as syllables and stress. You might have seen these symbols in dictionaries before, just next to the word itself.

Spellings in many languages often may not correspond with how the letters are pronounced, and as we noted earlier in this chapter, different languages have their own unique sets of sounds. The IPA was developed to tackle these very issues. It encompasses *all* possible sounds made by humans, and can, therefore, describe any word or any pronunciation.

So, for example, I can learn to pronounce the Spanish 'zapato' [θa.ˈpa.to] (shoe), the English 'conscience' [ˈkɒn.ʃ(ə)ns], the French 'enfant' [ˈɑ̃fɑ̃] (child), as well as words from other scripts, for example, the Tamil word 'பழக்கம்' [pa.ɻa.kkam] (habit).

Being able to read and use the IPA means that you can theoretically learn to pronounce any word in any language, without even knowing that language.

Worksheet 1

1. (a) Are there any sounds in your language you find difficult to pronounce when you talk fast? What about in a new language you are learning? Write them down here.

_____
_____
_____
_____

   (b) Write down a few words that have these sounds in them. Imagine you are giving these examples to a person trying to learn your language. Remember, in English, the sound may not correspond to the letters that make up the word (and the spelling often may not make any sense).

For example, words that have the 's' sound: **s**andwich, **c**elebrity, a**s**k, ca**s**tle, for**c**e, **c**ircle.

Here, the letter C can *also* have the 's' sound.

___

___

___

___

(c) What if I were to write 'dogs' or 'ends' or 'drawers'? Does the letter 'S' in these have the same 's' sound?

___

___

___

___

2. Have you ever noticed which part of the mouth you use to make certain sounds?

For example, for the sound 'p', notice that your lips are pressed together, and just as you open them, your breath is released, and the sound just...comes out! What about the sound 'b'? It's the same mouth movement! Why do you think the sounds come out different?

___

___

___

___

(a) We have given you eight sounds below, which are made by using different parts of your mouth, such as the lips, the tongue, the teeth, the roof of your mouth or the back of your throat. Say them out loud.

    i) 'm'   v) 'dha'

ii) 'l'   vi) 'r'
iii) 'w' vii) 'cha'
iv) 'p'   viii) 'g'

- Which parts of your mouth are used to make the sounds? (Remember that some sounds require two parts.)
- Does it sound nasal? (Y/N)
- Is your tongue touching another part? (Y/N)
- Can you feel air coming out of your mouth? (Y/N)

(b) What are some other sounds you can think of in your language? For example, both of us are fascinated by the Tamil sound that is most often transcribed as 'zha' in English.

_____
_____
_____
_____

(c) How do you pronounce your own name?

_____
_____

3. Let's try some sound associations.

Take the example of the sound 'z'. It could remind you of the words 'zoo' and 'zebra', and of the buzzing sound bees make, 'zzzzzz'. These associations will then remind you how to say the sound whenever you see a new word or are learning a new language. The Spanish word, 'zapato' (shoe)', or the Marathi word 'zadu' (broom), uses this very sound.

Another example is learning the slightly difficult 'z' sound in Urdu, through the ending sound in 'boys' or 'cheese'. Say 'boys' and then use the same 'z' sound to start the Urdu word 'zameen' (land).

Here is another example: To make the sound 'ch', the Hindi word 'chacha', or even the dance, cha-cha-chá, can be associated. It helps if you remember eating chikki in primary school, and liking the word 'chammach' (spoon). Associations are not just words but also any sensation or memory. Because of these associations, whenever Akhila hears the sound 'ch', she can pronounce it correctly.

Do you have any specific words that you immediately recall for a sound? Try listing at least two associations for the following sounds:

'd'

_____

_____

'aa'

_____

_____

'n'

_____

_____

'w'

_____

_____

4. Imagine you're teaching someone greetings in your first language. How will you mimic the pronunciation exaggeratedly?
Write down some of these words here.

_____

_____

_____

_____

5. A fun way to learn some new words and practise their pronunciation is through **tongue twisters**. A tongue twister is a phrase that is difficult to articulate or pronounce (especially without practice). Try some for yourself!
   - The sixth sick sheikh's sixth sheep's sick.
   - Nine nimble noblemen nibbling nuts.
   - Round the rough and rugged rock the ragged rascal rudely ran.

Before we move on to the next section, where sounds have meanings, let us recall that even when you don't know the meaning of a word or have never seen it before, you can often guess how to pronounce it.

Here is an example of one of the greatest 'nonsense' poems in the English language, 'Jabberwocky' by Lewis Carroll, from *Through the Looking-Glass*.[10] Read it aloud. Even though you don't know these words (a lot of them don't exist!), you automatically (and confidently) pronounce them in a certain way, don't you?

'Twas brillig, and the slithy toves
    Did gyre and gimble in the wabe:
All mimsy were the borogoves,
    And the mome raths outgrabe.

'Beware the Jabberwock, my son!
    The jaws that bite, the claws that catch!
Beware the Jubjub bird, and shun
    The frumious Bandersnatch!'

He took his vorpal sword in hand;

---

[10]Carroll, L., *Through the Looking-Glass*, Project Gutenberg, Urbana, IL, 2011. Retrieved 27 June 2018, from http://www.gutenberg.org/ebooks/12

> Long time the manxome foe he sought—
> So rested he by the Tumtum tree
>   And stood awhile in thought.
>
> And, as in uffish thought he stood,
>   The Jabberwock, with eyes of flame,
> Came whiffling through the tulgey wood,
>   And burbled as it came!
>
> One, two! One, two! And through and through
>   The vorpal blade went snicker-snack!
> He left it dead, and with its head
>   He went galumphing back.
>
> 'And hast thou slain the Jabberwock?
>   Come to my arms, my beamish boy!
> O frabjous day! Callooh! Callay!'
>   He chortled in his joy.
>
> 'Twas brillig, and the slithy toves
>   Did gyre and gimble in the wabe:
> All mimsy were the borogoves,
>   And the mome raths outgrabe.

Words and Phrases

Words are not simply strings of sounds, and not every string of sound means something. You can string together a series of sounds from a language, and they may mean nothing. I can make up nonsense words, such as 'claggable' or 'gimblon' or 'hooger'.

Words are only as important as the meaning ascribed to them. In our native language, we simply *know* meanings of words. If someone puts you on the spot and asks for the meaning of say, 'truth' or 'awkward' or 'listlessly', you may stutter and sputter and say you *know* it but can't really *explain* it. This just shows that while we may not have explicit knowledge of something, in our minds, we have made some associations to these words and we **implicitly understand** them.

This is one of the biggest challenges in learning new and foreign words. With the 'Jabberwocky' above, if you speak English, the words may stick in your memory simply because of how unusual they are.

However, in a new language, all the words are unusual, therefore, you need to be more careful and focus on the meaning, so that:

- It will remain longer in your mind.
- It will get associated with other words, so you will know how to use it next time.

To create strong associations in the mind, do the following:

- Pair it with a picture or memory (think of the Spanish word 'arroz', then think of a bowl of rice or *look* at a picture of rice when you say the word).
- Pair it with other words, either in the same language or other languages.

Sometimes, we may find that there are no words in our language to succinctly describe what we are feeling or doing. The beauty of learning a new language is that it gives you an entirely new vocabulary to express yourself. It fills you with wonder at the possibility of language.

Note: We often see lists of 'untranslatable words'. No word can be truly untranslatable because its meaning can still be conveyed. While some languages can describe complex phenomena in just one word, this cannot always be translated *easily*.

For example, the Japanese words 'komorebi' that means 'the sunshine that filters through leaves', and 'tsundoku' that means 'the act of leaving a book unread after buying, typically piling it up together with other unread books'. These are both single words used to express a whole concept. You can't find a corresponding *single* word in English. But you can still explain the meaning.

There is also the Hindi word 'jugaad'. Many argue that it has no simple translation. How will you explain this to a non-Hindi speaker? 'Making innovative adjustments to existing objects so you can solve problems' is not exactly very concise but might work. You may also need to supplement this with examples; like hanging bottles of ice-water in front of fans to mimic the effects of an AC. You are unlikely to forget the word 'jugaad' now.

The problem with words is there are so many of them. The English language alone has over 1,70,000 words. So, even if it is your first language, you are always going to encounter new words. However, not all words are used with equal frequency. That is, some words are used more often than others, and so it makes sense to first master the most frequently used ones which makes our job much simpler. A good place to start is online, where you can find word lists of the 100 or 1,000 most common words in many different languages.

Worksheet 2

1. Make a list of the first ten or fifteen words that you use every day in the language you speak in. For example, you

are sure to list the words for 'Good morning', 'Thank you' and 'Please'.

2. Think about a language you learnt in school or outside. What were the first words and sentences they taught you?

Listening—in context

One of the best ways to pick up words is to listen. You can do this by:

- Watching movies or TV shows in the language you want to learn or improve;
- Singing along to some music (movie songs are a great way to begin with);
- Striking up a conversation whenever you meet a speaker of that language. Introduce yourself and say you're learning that language.

You choose what interests you. There are people who like Japanese anime, K-pop music or Spanish telenovelas. You will find that these people would have automatically picked up some words, without even trying.

Going Pro

Whenever you come across a new word, ask the people to repeat it or rewind the track or dialogue. Some programmes on the computer allow you to slow down the speed of playback.

Be curious, look up the meaning and—most important of all—try them out for yourself. Saying them out loud will *actively* help you store the memory better, as opposed to *passively* just reading or listening. Activate your muscles. Add meaning. Use it in as many ways as possible.

Repetition + Chunking

As we said earlier, repetition is only one way of learning. When learning new or complicated words, however, you may not always be able to repeat them easily.

Take the word 'preliminary'. It is a big word. To those unfamiliar with the word (or even those who know it), trying to read it out loud, in one go, and repeating this, can be quite a tongue twister—just try saying it thrice in a row. Instead, it makes sense to break the word down, as you would pronounce it: pre-LIM-in-airy.

This breaking down of complex words into simpler, smaller bits is the same concept we saw earlier—**chunking.** It can be used not only to learn words but also longer phrases.

Regardless of the language, there are some common phrases you are likely to learn first:
'My name is _____';
'I am from _____';
'I like to _____ and _____ '; and so on.

When travelling to a new place, sometimes you just have to learn some basic phrases to get by. You may learn:

'How do you get from _____ to _____?'
'I don't speak any _____ !'
'How much does _____ cost?'

These phrases are immensely useful and you can make them more complex as your vocabulary improves.

Take the phrase, 'I want a pen'. Let us take 'I want' as one **chunk**.

Therefore, the sentence becomes 'I want _____.

This phrase can then be adapted to:

'I want a ball.'
'I want a toy.'
'I want a car.'

As your vocabulary grows, you can make the second part of the sentence more complex.

'I want to learn more German.'
'I want to go to the beach and swim.'

Alternatively, if you take 'want a pen' as your chunk, your sentences might become:

'He wants a pen.'
'They want a pen.'
'We want a pen.'

This requires an additional level of skill—the knowledge of how to conjugate (change) the verb 'want'. This technique allows you to even practise your tenses. And again, you can make more complex sentences:

'He wants a pen because he needs to write a letter.'

Often, this process happens unconsciously in our mother tongue. Nobody has to tell us how to use *each and every* word we come across. Just by listening to and reading the structure of sentences and how words are used, we often automatically deduce what to do.

When languages have different genders for objects—as in Marathi, where a chair is feminine ('tee khurchi'), or as in French, where a book is masculine ('le livre')—you may need to practise these sentences a little differently.

For example, French students are taught to **chunk** the gender along with the noun, so they know how to use it later. 'Le livre', 'la table', 'la télévision', etc.

In some languages, you may find that there are some patterns that words follow. Some chunks may be common across several words. In English, for example, you may find that you can sometimes find antonyms (opposites) of words by simply adding common prefixes, such as un-, mis-, dis-, im(-), etc.

Some examples are: appear (**dis**appear), order (**dis**order), patient (**im**patient), polite (**im**polite), available (**un**available), usual (**un**usual), and so on.

Some other common chunks in English (with examples) are: anti- (**anti**climax), bi- (**bi**lingual), non- (**non**sense), -ation (sens**ation**), -ible (sens**ible**), -ant (applic**ant**), and so on. Here, 'anti', 'bi' and 'non' are prefixes with fixed meaning, whereas we have added '-ation', '-ible' and '-ant' because they are usually pronounced the same way in whichever word they appear (think of loc**ation**, tang**ible**, dist**ant**, etc.).

The more you say it, the easier it becomes. The ultimate aim when learning a new language is to master this skill—learning to use words correctly in sentences without having to stop and think about where each word should go and how it should be used.

This cannot happen simply by writing in a language. Writing allows you to take a pause and think. **Fluency** can *only* happen by speaking. The process of speaking requires the brain to process information at an enormous speed.

Have you ever thought about how fast one must be thinking to be able to speak and produce the correct sounds and words in a continuous stream, and sometimes, while holding one or two other strains of thought simultaneously?

We discussed associations earlier in this chapter, but that was to help you with your pronunciation. The idea, however, is similar. When you want to learn a new word, try and form associations between it and another idea or concept already there in your mind. This method helps you remember not only the *sounds* but also the *meaning*.

For example, take the word 'phone'. The words that immediately come to my mind are: black, shiny, light, flat, number, message.

Therefore, when learning a new word, try and learn them **thematically**. This will connect similar ideas in your mind. You can also write down associations in a language you know (as we did above), and learn the translations for these. For example, if you had to learn the Hindi word 'billi' (cat), what are the immediate associations that come up in your mother tongue? Now, find the Hindi words for these associations. You can do this in any language.

Using Link Words

A related technique is that of **link words**. This is a mnemonic system to help connect similar-sounding words from different languages.

Take the Spanish word, 'arroz' (rice). 'Arroz' sounds a lot like the English word 'arrows'. So I would imagine someone shooting **arrows** into a sack of **rice**. This creates both a **phonetic** and **visual** association in the brain. Or take the Spanish word 'correr' (to run), which sounds like the English 'courier'. The image in my mind is now that of a courier running around, delivering packages. These are both words we have come across before: the first time, we learnt how to pronounce them; the second time, we learnt the meaning.

Of course, not all words have similarly equivalent-sounding counterparts in both your native language and your target language, but it is still a useful and fun technique to try. Make up stories and link back to what you know. Strong visuals and unusual associations form great connections in your brain.

Setting to Music

Many of you would have learnt the English alphabet with the nursery rhyme, learnt counting with 'Who stole a cookie from the cookie jar?' or learnt to distinguish between right and left with the Boogie Woogie song ('Put your right hand in, take your right hand out…'). If you are musically inclined, you could try this yourself. It is a great way to learn word lists and sentences.

You simply have to set the information to a simple-but catchy melody, and keep humming away. Songs have a way of sticking in the mind. (Ever heard of an earworm? Look it up.) When the time comes to revise the information, you simply have to sing.

In fact, you might already find yourself humming sentences set to a popular film song when you're bored. (For instance, once when Akhila was waiting for someone to come down in the lift, she found herself singing, 'Come down, we're getting laaaaate…' in operatic style!)

An interesting example of this is when Sonu Nigam, the Hindi singer, once tried to explain how songs are made by using the phrase 'aaloo, mooli, gobi, mutter paneer' set to various popular tunes. Even if you heard this only once, these five food items will never be forgotten.

The Method of Loci

This is one of the most powerful memory tools. The Method of Loci is nothing but an extension of the idea of association. If you remember from Chapter 3, the word 'locus' (plural: loci) means position. Therefore, this method involves imagining the locations of information.

So, how does it work?

Imagine a familiar place. Take your home for instance. Imagine the route from the main door to your bedroom, and then imagine yourself walking there. Now, at the foot of your door, imagine yourself placing a word there—any word that you want to remember. Suppose, it is the word 'bulldoze', imagine the word lying at your doorstep. Go a step further and imagine a yellow, beeping **bulldozer** trying to break the door down. The more vivid (or bizarre) the imagery, the more likely it is to stick. This way, you will also learn to connect and remember the **meaning** of the word, and not just the word itself.

Now, as you walk through your house, place words along this path—on a chair, a table, in a bowl, or hanging on the wall. Then as we did earlier, create an image or imagine a sensation connecting the two: the word and the area.

Here's another example: let's place the word 'boisterous' inside a shoe by the door. The two words have seemingly no connection, but the challenge is to be creative. How about imagining little dust mites going absolutely wild inside a dark and damp **shoe**, bouncing off the sides **boisterously**. That's a pretty strange image.

Remember: where memory is concerned, STRANGE = MEMORABLE.

It can be a fun exercise to do this. One by one, place these words in familiar places in your head, this will become your **mind place**—a place for you to store and lock away information for later. Walk through this imaginary space, whether it is your classroom, or the beach or your bathroom, as often as you can, to strengthen these associations. Make them more and more vivid; add colours, smells, tastes and sounds. Soon, you will see that you're remembering whole lists of words.

We can also add a twist to the Method of Loci. If you're learning a new language, you could try this in your actual bedroom to learn simple vocabulary.

Imagine your bedroom and all the objects in it. Now, imagine walking around and touching each item. Or, if you're in your room, you can even do it by physically walking around and touching each item. As you touch each item, say the name of that item in the new language.

Let's look at how this would work in French, with an example from Akhila:

*When I think of my room, I imagine my **bed**, my **table**, my **books**.*

Now, in my mind, I am imagining walking around my room and touching these objects. As I touch the bed, I say, 'le lit'. As I touch the table, I say, 'la table'. As I touch the books, I say, 'les livres'.

This is a great way to add vocabulary to memory. And it's so easy to practise. When you are bored or have some free time, close your eyes, imagine the room and try to name all the objects in it using the new language. You can imagine walking up to them in a different order each time.

If you are in the space, walking around physically and saying the words out loud is a way to make it even more memorable. You can do this with any room or space: your classroom, your living room, your friend's house, a restaurant that you visit often, or even with the contents of your bag.

Once you can recall all the names without any mistake, you can make more complex sentences by mixing them up. For example, The book **is on** the table. The bed is **next to** the table.

Going Pro: See if you can describe these objects (colour, size, shape, etc.) in that language. Do you know the words for different adjectives?

These are some words you could use to describe them:
Bed: flat, comfortable, wooden;
Cupboard: metallic, rectangular, empty;
Book: interesting, old.

Taking this *even* further, you can learn action words. How do you use this object? What can it do? What other action words would you associate with these objects?

Bed: Sleep (I *sleep* on the bed), Sit (I *sit* on the bed);
Cupboard: Open (I *open* the cupboard), Slam (I *slammed* the cupboard door shut);
Book: Read (I *read* the book), Forgot (I *forgot* about the book).

Some more advanced activities can even be used to improve vocabulary in your L1. For example, to describe your cupboard: 'It is **vintage**. It has elaborate **fretwork** on the door. The material is **unyielding**.' Just visualize clearly and associate the words with the image in your head.

The final technique we are going to suggest is also one

of the most fun and dramatic ways of listening to something and using it to improve speaking.

Roleplay

If you are learning a new language with your friends or in a classroom, this gives you plenty of opportunity to practise your speaking skills. A simple and commonly used exercise in these situations is **roleplay.**

Roleplay is nothing but acting by improvisation. Usually, your teacher gives you a situation or you can choose a situation and the teacher asks you to imagine a conversation.

These can be two-person conversations, like when you are buying something in a shop, asking for directions from someone, or making plans for later. You can also do this in a larger group, discuss a movie you all watched recently, or pretend you're all old friends catching up after many years.

When you are slightly more confident about vocabulary and grammar, you can try out more adventurous situations.

What if you could be Batman and the Joker confronting each other? Or, what if you're all hatching some conspiracy? Or, you're all lost in the forest and have to survive together? The possibilities are endless, and in the process, you work on your acting skills as well. The best thing is, when you're working in a situation like this in a group, you forget to be scared. And when discussing things with people, they often add new vocabulary, or something they say may remind *you* of some word you have learnt earlier and can then share it with the group.

This method can also be combined with one of the methods we learnt above to practise your pronunciations: imitating films and television shows, or your favourite actors and characters.

Tuning in to films and TV shows is a great way to pick up new words, sounds and phrases. Say the lines with the same intonation and gusto as the character in the movie or show. Add in actions that suit the words—imagine yourself to be a mighty warrior or a stealthy spy. Your mind will connect the words to the action, and you will have more associations with the word or phrase.

If you want to talk clearly, imagine you are a diplomat in the United Nations or an MP making a speech in the parliament. The speech can be about anything. It can be about how there should be more sports in school, or how you deserve holidays to watch your favourite movies. Just be careful to speak loudly, clearly and dramatically. Above all, have fun.

Remember, always ask for help if you need it. There's no point in getting stuck or learning something wrong and having to unlearn it. Ask your teacher or a friend, look it up online or in a dictionary. You do not have to do this alone.

Worksheet 3

1. Look up some famous film or television dialogues from a language you want to learn.

    Here are five famous dialogues from English films:

    'I' am gonna make him an offer he can't refuse.' Don Corleone (*The Godfather*)
    'It's levi-O-sa, not levi-o-SA!' Hermione (*Harry Potter and the Philosopher's Stone*)
    'My precious…!' Gollum (*The Lord of the Rings*)
    'We're not in Kansas anymore!' Dorothy (*The Wizard of Oz*)
    'Luke, I am your father.' Darth Vader (*Star Wars*)

Look them up if you haven't heard them before. You will notice that all of these are said rather exaggeratedly, in different voices and accents. These are perfect for trying yourself—imitate the line exactly as you hear it—intonation, expressions and all.

2. Here is an English sentence: 'I go to the shop'.

   The sentence can be broken down into: I go to the shop.

   Based on what we learnt about chunking, see if you can come up with different versions using different chunks of this sentence.

   I go to ––––––––––––––––––––––––– .

   For example: I go to my friend's house.

   ––––––––––––––––– go to the shop.

   For example: We go to the shop.

   ––––––––––––– the shop.

   For example: Philip cycled to the shop.

3. Here is the beginning of a story.

   Where is everyone? Poor Aditi watched as the train pulled out of the station. She had been waiting for her friends for half an hour, but there was no sign of them. And now, because of them, she had missed the train. Oh, why hadn't she thought to get her own copy of the ticket! They had been planning this trip for months. She was really looking forward to it.

   She waited another ten minutes, sighed, and picked up her bags to head back home. Out of the corner of her eye, she saw someone running towards her and yelling, 'Did we make it? Where's the train!' The others joined in one by one behind her. They soon realized what had happened.

   Now, try and act out the rest of the story from here, by yourself, or in a group. Where do you think they were going? What do you think they are going to do now? Do you think they can still salvage the trip?

Remember: try to be as animated as possible. How would you feel if you'd just missed a train? Would you just give up and go home? What would you tell your friends?

4. Imagine your classroom in school. You must be familiar with it; you spend so much time there. Now, picture the room—the colours on the wall, the positioning of the desks and chairs, the blackboard, the fans, the clock, the windows—all of it.

Here is a list of six words:

Solitaire
Bulbous
Elegant
Sequester
Cartwheel
Intimidating

Using the Method of Loci, place these words in the classroom in your mind, and try and create associations between the location and the word. If you do not know the meanings of these words, ask someone for help, or look them up.

Here is an example: 'I placed "elegant" on the blackboard, because my teacher has elegant handwriting.'

Write down your associations here, as simply as you can. After rehearsing this mentally twice, can you close the book and remember all the words?

_____
_____
_____
_____
_____
_____

Difficult Sounds

When learning to speak, listening is extremely important. Whenever possible, try listening to a native speaker pronounce sounds that are unique to that language.

For example, in Marathi, the letter 'च' ('ch') is pronounced in two completely different ways.

In the Marathi word 'chandra' (moon), the 'ch' is pronounced as in the English word 'chum'. But the word for star is 'chandani', where the 'ch' has no real English equivalent but is closest to the sound in 'tzar' or the sound when you make the disapproving sound 'tch tch'! However, they are both written using the same letter, as you can see:

चन्द्र (moon)
चांदणी (star)

If you are learning Marathi for the first time, you will need to associate these sounds with as close an approximation as possible in languages you already speak. But, you will benefit most from listening to native speakers pronouncing these sounds and trying to mimic them until your tongue falls into the right position naturally.

FIVE

Reading and Writing

In Chapter 2, we discussed how children are born ready to **speak**. They spend the first year of their life learning to form words and speak, by simply paying attention to and copying people around them. If you recall, we specified that this was true for all children. Children with hearing or speech impairments still do this; they simply use hand gestures when exposed to this stimulus by people around them.

However, reading and writing in *any* language is quite a different matter from speaking. No child needs to be taught to babble. But no child is born ready to learn to read, and their hand muscles are not developed enough to be able to write for at least two or three years. Reading and writing are two skills that all children need to be explicitly **taught**; they can't be **acquired** from the environment.

The journey from speaking to reading and writing takes time. This is because your brain has to recognize that the signs on a page correspond to the sounds you are making. And very often, the way sounds are written is not consistent.

For example, can you think of three different sounds the letters 'g' and 'h' make together?

The words 'ghost', 'daughter' and 'laughter' are a case in point. How would you explain to someone who is just learning to read English that the *same* letters are pronounced so differently everywhere?

Or take the letter '*A*'. It is pronounced differently in '**d**am', '**d**ame' and '**d**ance'. How confusing!

In fact, in many languages, the written and spoken forms are themselves quite different. Again English is one of the best examples of this: 'laughter' is pronounced 'LAAF-ter'; 'psychology' is pronounced 'sai-KAW-luh-jee' and 'knowledge' is pronounced 'NAW-lij', to name just a few.

Not all languages have these wide differences, of course. But because English is made up of words from so many different languages (Greek, Latin, Germanic—to name just three influences), it has more spelling variations to match all the languages in its history.

There is a very famous example, even cited by George Bernard Shaw, that demonstrates how mixed up English is.

'GHOTI'. Yes, Ghoti. What word do you think this is?

Ghoti = Fish.

How, you may ask? The answer to this is at the end of the chapter. Think of the example we've given for spelling variations in English, and you can come up with your own as well. Be as creative as you like.

Before we move on to techniques to help you improve your reading and understanding of a language, let's quickly look at why reading and writing are so special.

Reading and Writing: Signs and Sounds

অ ੫ ഞ И ఠఄఄ థ

Look at the alphabets above. Do you recognize any of these shapes? You might think some of them look familiar, or you might even know some of them because you speak those languages.

Yes, these are letters from different language scripts. From left to right, you have letters from Japanese, Persian, Malayalam, Russian, Kannada and Bengali.

We specified left to right because in some languages are read from right to left. And traditionally, Chinese, Japanese and Korean are read from top to bottom.

Now, let's begin with the L1 (mother tongue, in everyday terms). We learn to speak it and then someone shows us a picture of an apple. There are some 'designs' below the picture that look like this:

A P P L E

As a young child, these designs look as random as some of the shapes on the previous page look to you.

Slowly, with the help of parents and teachers, children learn that each 'design', is associated with a sounds.

For example:

A is associated with an 'aah' sound;

P is associated with a 'puh' sound.

And so on, until they learn and start remembering the sounds associated with different letters.

Once we become proficient at reading, we often forget some of the things that we found confusing as beginners in a language. But confusions abound, especially with reading and writing. In some languages, the same letter can be associated with two sounds.

For example, in English, 'C' can be pronounced as a 's' (as in 'trace') or a 'k' sound (as in 'car').

In Tamil, the same letter, 'ட', can be pronounced as a hard 'da' (as in 'dog') or hard 'ta' (as in 'top') and you need to know which sound it represents in that word.

Further, there are three ways of writing the 'na' sound in Tamil and you have to know which letter corresponds to the sound you are choosing.

So, when they start reading, children start by learning simple sounds at first. They then slowly start putting them together, in small words, then in more complex words.

So, they know that 'CUT' is made up of a 'kuh', an 'uh' and a 'tuh' sounds. But what about words like 'cuticle'? The child has to learn how the different sounds go together.

They also have to then recognize that these sounds correspond to words they have been saying all along. After all, many children can say 'computer', but even after they learn the letters, it may take them some time to understand that the sounds conveyed by the letters C O M P U T E R are the same as the word they use so often.

Anyone who has learnt a second language with a different writing system (Hindi, Malayalam, Russian, Greek, etc.) knows how difficult it is to learn letters that are not there in your first language. It's even more difficult when there are new sounds, as we discussed in the previous chapter.

All of this is being reiterated to remind you that even your own mother tongue was learnt over three or four or even five years. So, do not be discouraged when learning a new language takes time.

Plus, even in your first language, you will continue to discover new words, proverbs and idioms throughout your life. What is important is being open to learning new facts and having a good foundation. That way, when a new word comes along, you can quickly connect it to two or three other related concepts and thus, anchor it in your long-term memory or semantically process it, so it gets stored well.

Writing is similar, yet different. While reading, you are learning to recognize signs. In writing, you have to draw those signs by yourself and also learn how to correctly spell the words. Go back and look at your notebooks from pre-school, or even from the first or second standard. Compare your handwriting and speed of writing back then to the same now. Isn't there a vast difference?

You will face the same difference when learning a new language. Initially, you may be slow or your handwriting may not be clear and legible. But as it was in school, your handwriting changes with time, and your speed also improves significantly.

Some languages share a script, so it is easier to learn them if you already know one. English, French, German, etc. use the same letters. So do Marathi, Hindi and Sanskrit (with one or two extra letters in each language). This way you can quickly **transfer** learning.

Transfer of learning is, very simply, what happens when something you have learnt earlier influences something you are learning now.

For example, if you speak Tamil and are learning Kannada, you will recognize the words for 'above' and 'below' (as they are very similar to Tamil). You will, thus, recall these words more quickly and use them correctly. This is your learning from **an L1** transferring to **the L2**.

But why is writing in any script important at all?

Writing is important because you are forming **muscle memories.** As we have seen before, when your muscles perform the same actions again and again, muscle memories are formed, which means that your body basically remembers how to do things *automatically*.

Think about using your computer. Your fingers automatically know how to click on the mouse and your hand knows what pressure to use to move the mouse around. You may even instinctively know where the keys on your keyboard are. All this is what we call muscle memory.

Can you guess why muscle memory is important to writing? This is because when you write the same thing over and over again, your muscles remember the movements. This way, you learn the shapes of the letters and also the spellings of the most common words easily.

Exercise

Here are three words. Remember them by using one of the memory techniques we saw earlier for learning words.
Tree
Three
Tyrant
Now, close the book and write down all three words.

What did you find? Did you write the first two words quicker than you wrote the last word? This might be because they are more commonly used and your hand is used to writing them, whereas for 'tyrant', you know the letters but your muscles may not remember writing that word as frequently.

As you can see, writing is one of the best ways to **encode** words in your brain. The more you write in a language, the more natural it will seem to you.

But what about technology? Well, looking up things online is great, but where writing is considered, using your hand still seems like a good way of learning.

Typing is not as efficient for learning, especially for spellings. One of the reasons is that most devices you type on have Autocorrect features. So, you don't even realize what mistake you have made, as the computer or phone quickly corrects it for you.

However, when you write on paper and make corrections, there are three reasons that the correct words may stay longer:

1. Muscle memory;
2. Effort and meaning: according to the Levels of Processing theory (from Chapter 1), the more you **process** information, the better it is encoded. With writing, you are putting in effort and you are also thinking and focussing more on what you need to put down. As writing takes more time, it also gives you more time to learn and reflect;
3. When we write, especially in a different language, we are strengthening the connections in our mind between the letters and the sounds. Reading and writing are strongly linked.

Indeed, in a study, one group of people were asked to type out words or letters from new alphabets, while another group was asked to write the same ones.[11] Researchers found that the people who wrote down the letters tended to remember them better than those who typed out the same ones. This is especially important if you are learning a new script.

Another study that compared handwriting with keyboard typing or writing on a device, such as an iPad, still found that writing worked best.[12]

Memory—Reading—Writing

Nowadays, everyone is familiar with these terms, thanks to computer memory (where you can Read data or Write data). But let's look at this in human terms. What is the best way

---

[11] Mangen, Anne, Anda, Liss, H. Oxborough, Gunn and Brønnick, Kolbjørn, 'Handwriting versus Keyboard Writing: Effect on Word Recall', *Journal of Writing Research*, 7(2):227–47, 2015. Available at 227-247. 10.17239/jowr-2015.07.02.1. (accessed in 2018)

[12] Ibid.

to read and write so that you can remember words and use them later?

Reading and writing are essential, even in your first language. New words and new styles are all important and contribute to keeping your memory engaged and sharp.

Further, the best way to progress in any language (including your L1) is to read. Read widely: novels, magazines, Wikipedia entries, or even instruction manuals. Can you guess why?

Exposure to more and more writing will help you internalize the grammar of the language that you are reading. You will begin to understand in what order to put the nouns and adjectives; you can understand how to use long sentences and also learn new idioms and phrases.

Graphic novels or comics are excellent ways to learn a new language. The illustrations are always helpful and the stories are fun and full of adventure or mystery, and often quite humorous. Try them out.

Reading Comprehension

Have you noticed how, in your language exams, you are asked to read a text and then answer questions about it? This is called **Reading Comprehension** and is an important part of language use. Leaving aside the learning of new words, one of the most important parts of communication is to understand what is being said to you. The only way this can be done is if your brain has stored patterns—either vocal or images, so it can understand what someone else is trying to say.

Every time you listen to a song, a news report or a movie dialogue, you are using memory. Your brain is processing the sounds coming in and matches them to the information that is stored. It, then, derives meaning from these sounds or fills in the blanks.

For example, imagine that you and your friend are in a crowded train and you hear your friend say, 'Let's get_____at the next stop. I want_____eat, I'm very_____.' Now, you couldn't hear some words, but based on whatever else you heard and also earlier conversations and uses of words, you think that the most logical explanation is that your friend said, 'Let's get <u>out</u> at the next stop. I want <u>to</u> eat. I'm very <u>hungry</u>.'

Similarly, whenever you read, your brain has to do the same thing. It must remember the letters, what they signify and then give you the meaning. In a few cases, you may even remember the order of specific words and guess words that come next.

For example, if you see a notice that starts off, 'BEWARE OF...' and the next part of it is hidden/missing, you will recall other such notices you have seen in the past and automatically fill in the blanks. What do you think follows here?

So, while reading or listening to comprehension questions in a language exam may seem pointless, they are, in fact, testing your ability to understand communications in that language. And you cannot do this without your brain using memories to recognize, organize and interpret information.

Reading: Active Participation

One of the first and most important techniques to read in any language is to read *aloud*. This helps you improve pronunciation and gives you a clear idea about the connection between the words and the corresponding sounds. Children are encouraged to read aloud and it's also a great tactic for people of any age learning new languages.

Roleplaying could be added on to this tactic for even more fun! One of our favourite techniques when trying to learn a text or a new language is to pretend that we are native speakers—perhaps, even important dignitaries.

Let us take the example of Hindi.

As discussed in the previous chapter, one fun way of learning pronunciation is to pretend that you are a famous movie star and to try and repeat their actions and diction.

We propose a similar game here but with a text. Take a text and then pretend, for example, that you are Amitabh Bachchan and you are trying to teach someone Hindi. How would you then read the text? Would you race through it? Or, read it carefully and clearly?

Read the text, be slow and clear, so that an imaginary audience can catch every word. Never mind if you make mistakes. Go back and read the line and correct yourself.

Perhaps you are Amitabh Bachchan reading a script for the first time. Imagine that you are explaining this text to your audience.

Now, when you try to convey the meaning of the text, you first need to understand it yourself. This requires **deep processing**, which, as we have seen, ensures that information is better coded. Also, by reading it slowly and clearly, you are ensuring that your brain understands the connections between the letters and the sounds.

You can add another element to this roleplaying, even if you're not being any specific actor: read the text with as much expression as possible. That is, add in as much emotion and *drama* as you can. Pretend it's a speech in a movie or a play, or you're a lawyer reading this text in court.

Exercise:

Here's a task. Read out the following text, adding as much expressiveness and emotion as you can:

'How dare you!' Tara screamed. She ran angrily towards the

people beating the dog. Everyone got scared and moved back. Tara was a small girl. But she was furious! She glared at all the people and then bent over the dog. The dog looked up sadly.

'Oh, you poor darling!' she cried and took the dog and hugged it tightly. The dog seemed so happy to find someone who cared for it!

Have you done it? You can even add actions if you want. Now, try and answer the questions without going back to the text:

1. What was the girl's name? _____
2. How tall was the girl? _____
3. What was happening? Why did Tara get angry?

_____
_____

Were you able to answer all the above three questions?

Doing something dramatic makes it *unusual*. And you tend to remember unusual things. Also, adding action and emotion to a story may give it more meaning.

But you can't just read it out with random emphases or emotions (anger, sorrow, etc.). You need to understand the text and then read it with the appropriate emotions. In this way, the gist of what you are reading is likely to remain with you longer.

Of course, not every text is likely to be so dramatic. If you are doing a school lesson on farming, in your second or third language, you may not be able to read the list of crops with much drama.

But in this case, take on an appropriate role. Imagine you are a farmer, talking about crops and what crops you grow in your region. Pretend that you're the expert and you need people to understand what is happening. Instead of focussing on expression, focus on being clear and decide which facts to stress upon.

Remember in the previous chapter when we asked you to pretend you were at the UN? Roleplaying with a text is similar but instead of making up a dialogue, a text is provided for you.

Words in Context or Using a Dictionary

Now, while reading, you *will* come across several words that you don't know, especially in a new language. How do you deal with that? There are two steps that we would recommend:

- Look at the previous sentence and the next one. Based on this context, can you guess the meaning of the word?
- Once you have guessed, immediately verify your guess using a physical dictionary or by searching online.

For example, here is a Tamil word in the middle of an English sentence. Can you guess the meaning of the word?

'Anita walked in and looked for her paati. There she was, her white hair shining in the sunlight, as she read a magazine. "Paati, I'm home. Is there anything to eat?" Her paati looked up and smiled, "Of course, child. Come. Your mother called. She's coming home late tonight."'

Now, based on this context, can you guess what 'paati' means? (The answer is given below, don't worry!) Let's try it with another word, a French word this time.

'Pierre was learning English and would usually speak fluently. But when he was tired or excited, French would often slip in. One day, he was talking to Maria and was very frustrated about his work.

"I was working on my ordinateur this morning but I forgot

to save my file and there was a power cut. Everything vanished."

Maria looked confused. "Your…what?"

"My ordinateur…oh sorry. I mean, my _____."

What do you think goes in the blank?

Now in the first text, what did you guess 'paati' was? From the text and description, you must have guessed that the word had something to do with the old lady. And she seemed to know Anita and her mother, and called Anita 'child'. Based on all this, did you guess that 'paati' means 'grandmother' in Tamil? If so, you were absolutely right!

And in the second text, you knew that Pierre was working on something. He forgot to save his work and lost it during the power cut. Can you think of how many things require electricity and can save files? If you guessed that 'ordinateur' means 'computer' in French, you are absolutely correct!

These texts are quite easy, of course. And you might not always find texts this easy, but if you try and focus on the surrounding words, you will always be able to guess at the general meaning. Here's another example:

'I was in Turkey last week with my family. I had a great time!'

'Turkey! My uncle is from there! I still remember the first time he got me some ayran.'

'Oh! Ayran! I loved it. It was so great.'

'I know! Especially on a hot day.'

Now, based on this conversation, what kind of substance do you think 'ayran' is? Clothes, food or drink?

Given the conversation, it is most probably something to eat or drink. We also know that it's great on a hot day, so it is most probably something cold.

Now that we have been able to figure out this much information, it's time to search through a dictionary. One of the best ways to look up new words is either in a physical dictionary, or by googling them.

Since it's highly unlikely that you have a Turkish dictionary lying around in case you come across a Turkish word somewhere, let's use Google.

If you type 'ayran+Turkey', this is what you get. You don't even need to read the text—just looking at the picture gives you a good idea of what it is. When you read the text, you understand that it is a drink that is just like lassi, or buttermilk, something you might have guessed from the picture.

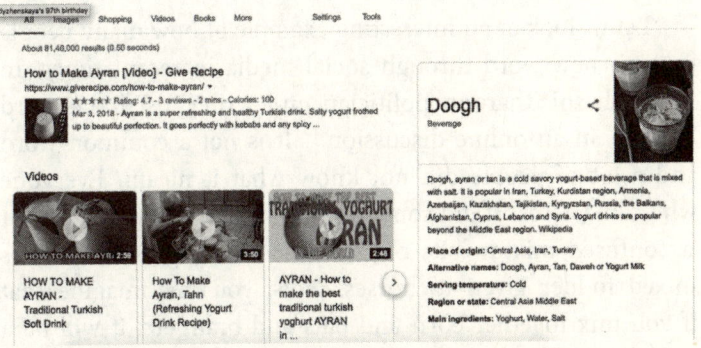

So, if you are reading a text, look up the meaning of new words. But first, try and guess the meaning in its context. Then, verify this information using a physical dictionary or the Internet.

However, just looking up this meaning or looking at a picture is not enough. Although, it will definitely help you remember the word better, in order to ensure that the word or expression is stored in your long-term memory, you need to reuse it, so that you know absolutely how the word is used and in what situations you can use it.

When you come across a new word, try and look up the meaning immediately. This way you can recall the context and reread that section with greater meaning and more interest. If you wait till later, you may forget the context and the word will be harder to store away. You may even forget to look it up altogether.

Also, taking the effort to look up the word either in a physical dictionary or on the Internet ensures that it holds more meaning, since you are taking more time to do it.

The Internet is also great for this, as you can see the images related to the word, which helps your brain store the information better.

Let us look at an interesting example of how many people learnt a new word through social media in recent times. In 2017, Shashi Tharoor, politician and writer, used the word 'farrago' in an online discussion.[13] It is not a common word and a lot of people did not know what it meant. Everyone who came across it did some research and learnt that it meant 'a confused mixture'. Its original use/meaning was that it is mixed fodder given to horses. Now, you can imagine that if you mix together corn and oats and bran, etc. it will be a mixture that is hard to separate.

Thus, a farrago is a very confused mixture of items.

Now, when this unusual word became so popular, many people on the Internet used it as a joke. For example, you could say, 'I had my Maths paper yesterday. It was so confusing! Just a **farrago** of random facts and figures!'

As we said before, by reusing the word, you are actually giving it more meaning. And thanks to all the jokes on the Internet, 'farrago' was a word that most people who read it still remember a few years later.

---

[13] https://twitter.com/ShashiTharoor/status/861608665517895680 (accessed in 2018)

This is certainly one of the best ways to learn and remember new words. As soon as you find out the meaning of a new word, **sit down and make three different sentences with the word**. Do not stop until you have at least three complete sentences.

Group tip: If you are working in a group, one fun thing will be to write two sentences each and then exchange them. You can then read each other's sentences out loud.

Can you think of a way to combine all the information and tips we have looked at so far?

Yes! **Write** the new word in different sentences, so it forms muscle memory and you have great meaning attached to it. Then **read out** your sentences, perhaps with actions or gestures. Do this right away with a new word you encountered today. (If you have not, look up a new word at random in a dictionary.)

_____
_____
_____

Worksheet

1. Here are three unusual words (one was used before). If you don't know the meaning of any of them, look it up in a dictionary (either physical or online). If you look it up online, you can also easily find examples of how to use them. Can you come up with three different sentences for *each* word? Try not to take more than three or four minutes per word. So, in total, about twelve minutes for all of them.

    (a) Farrago

    _____
    _____
    _____

(b) Hullabaloo

_____

_____

_____

(c) Pulchritude

_____

_____

_____

(If you don't know the meaning of 'pulchritude', it might surprise you! It surprised Akhila, when she first learnt it, because the word *looks* so different from what it means!)

2. Find three new words in a language that you want to learn (or, are learning). Do the same exercise. Write down three different sentences for each word. Make the sentences as varied as possible.

_____

_____

_____

Using New Vocabulary: Creating Stories

When we use words to link information together, we create stories. Making associations with meaning will help you remember the information. Don't be afraid to be silly or dramatic—the more gripping the information, the better it will be stored.

All you have to do is to create **links** or **associations** between words. Your brain remembers **images** and meaningful information.

Let's take an example using English words. Assume you want to learn the following five words:

Verbose, Luminous, Epiphany, Scurrilous, Frivolous

We thought about this and came up with the following story:

*A very **verbose** man, with a large, **luminous** head, had an **epiphany** when he realized that his stories were **scurrilous** and insulting and also **frivolous** and unimportant.*

Tell yourself the story a couple of times. **Imagine** a very talkative man, with a large bald and shiny head, stopping and having a surprising realization...

Can you see this image?

Always try and make stories out of things that are easy to imagine, so you are associating **words** and **images**.

As you can see, in the story above, in a couple of places, the word we want to learn is also followed by another word that has a similar meaning. This way you can easily remember the meaning or context and thus, be able to use the new word appropriately and correctly.

Writing New Scripts: Associating with the Older Ones

One of the most interesting things about learning new languages is learning new letters and sounds. However, this can also be confusing initially, especially when the letters are new or there are sounds that you are not very familiar with.

Let us consider French. It is written using Roman letters, like English. But the alphabet is different. In English, when you recite the alphabet, you say 'Ay, Bee, Cee, Dee...' etc.

In French, you recite the alphabet like this: 'Aah, Bey, Say, Dey.' Plus, the sounds of the letters *G* and *J* are interchanged with respect to English. One way of solving this problem is to associate the sounds with the sounds and letters from other languages you know (**transfer of learning**). This way, your mouth automatically knows what shape to take when reading those letters.

Here is an example using both Hindi and Tamil to remember the French alphabet:

French	Hindi	Tamil
A	आ	ஆ
B	बे	பெ
C	से	சே
D	दे	தே
E	अ	அ

However, you have to be careful that the language you are associating it with has the specific sounds. As we have mentioned before, not all languages have the same sounds.

Let us take the example of the *R* in French. It is a sound that does not exist in Tamil or Hindi *or* English. So, what we do is, we provide a *description* of that sound:

R = airh/air-gh

Each person will have a different way of remembering the sounds. This same letter may be written slightly differently by someone else (as you will see below). What is important is that when you write them down, you can *easily* associate the right sounds with the right words.

For example, you can learn the French alphabet (pronunciation) using only English. This is the list Akhila made when she was first learning French.

English	French	English	French
A	Aah	N	N
B	Bae	O	O
C	Say	P	Pay
D	They	Q	Kiu
E	Uh	R	Airrh/Errgh*
F	Ef	S	S

English	French	English	French
G	Jhay	T	Tay
H	Aash	U	Yiu
I	Ee	V	Whey
J	Jee	W	Doobluwhey
K	Ka	X	Iks
L	L	Y	Igrek
M	M	Z	Zed

*As you can see, Akhila writes the sound slightly differently from the student who gave the earlier description of 'airh/air-gh'.

Now, just reading this out, I'm pretty sure you have a good idea of what the French alphabet sounds like. This is not ideal, but it's a good beginning.

Here's Meghna's list for Spanish. Can you pronounce all the alphabets?

Alphabet	Pronunciation	Alphabet	Pronunciation
A	Aah	Ñ	Enye
B	Beh	O	Oh
C*	Seh	P	Peh
D	They	Q	Ku
E	Eh	R	Ere
F	Efe	S	Ese
G*	Hheh	T	The
H	Ache	U	Oo
I	I	V	Beh
J*	Hhotha	W	Doble ve
K	Ka	X	Ekis
L	Ele	Y	Ee griega
M	Eme	Z*	Seta/Zeta
N	Ene		

*The letters C, J, G and Z are pronounced in a way that has no real equivalent in English. This was Meghna's initial list to help her get her mouth in approximately the right shape. But these letters needed extra practice for her to accurately pronounce them and her initial notes don't give a perfect idea of their sound.

Writing: Fonts and Doodles

Besides writing and muscle memory, let us take a look at one more way in which we can use pen and paper to improve memory. All of us take notes—either shopping lists, or important points in some chapter, or some message to pass on to others.

But how can we ensure that these notes remain in our memory even when they are not immediately in front of us? One way is to make the writing itself **dramatic**.

See? That was an example right there. When something is in bold, you tend to pay more attention to it. And, as we have seen, when you pay more attention to something, you are likelier to store it in your short-term memory and then it can move to your long-term memory, if you rehearse it.

Let us look at **colours, fonts** and **doodles**. Do you remember being asked to use different colour pens to highlight points in your exam paper? Do you use different sketch pens when making notes?

Using colours is a great way to make something look unusual or to highlight it. Here are two examples:

Chennai's Marina Beach is not the world's second longest beach.

Chennai's Marina Beach is not the world's second longest beach.

Now, both these sentences are exactly the same. But depending on which one you are shown, you are likelier to remember different words.

So, the trick here is to put down important information in as unusual a form as you can. Use fancy fonts, bright colours, or just draw shapes around words and ideas. Something like this:

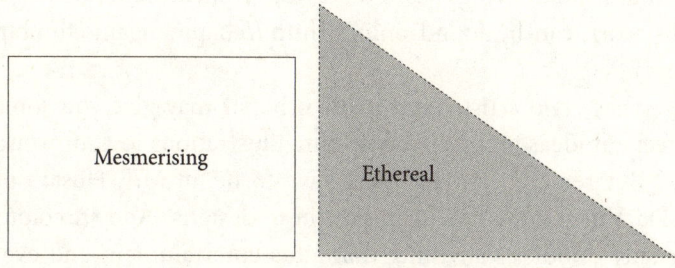

Another interesting trick, depending on how much you enjoy doodling, is to try and illustrate your work. You could use quirky images or literal drawing. Here's an illustration by Bengaluru-based artist, Harini Kannan, indicating three versions of a proverb. As you can see, the basic idea is the same (to accomplish two goals by taking one step). But the examples used in different languages are different.

Source: Harini Kannan

Another artist called James Chapman makes many interesting doodles and drawings based on sayings from around the world. His work can be found online (http://chapmangamo.tumblr.com).

These two artists (and many others!) may give you some excellent ideas for creatively adding illustrations to your work.

But remember—you don't have to be an M.F. Husain or a Da Vinci to be able to make these designs. Add in colour or silly doodles—anything that adds entertainment and eye-catching designs for *you*.

Your language notes are personal, unless you *want* to share them. Be as creative and silly as you like.

GHOTI: Do you remember the riddle we posed earlier?

Did you figure out how 'Ghoti' could be the same as 'Fish'? The logic used in the riddle is that these letters have specific sounds when used in different words (for example lauGH—wOmen—naTIon).

If you link these sounds together, they make up the sound of the word 'Fish'. Again, this was used simply to poke fun at English spellings and pronunciations and illustrate how confusing they can be!

> **Vocabulary Alert!**
>
> While, using similarities between languages can help you identify and store memories of new sounds and words better, there is also one danger you must avoid.
>
> **False cognates** are words that are spelt the same in different languages but have completely different meanings. You may have come across this yourself.
>
> (The word 'cognate' means 'related' or 'connected', therefore, a *false* cognate is a word that you *think* may

be similar in different contexts but in reality, they have a different meaning entirely).

One example of this is 'LOCATION' in English and French.

In English, the word means the 'position' of something, indicating where it can be found. 'What is your exact location now?' is something we often ask. And, of course, thanks to online maps, people can easily find most locations on their browser.

However, in French, if you asked someone for a 'LOCATION', you would mostly likely be given a number. This is because, in French, 'LOCATION' means 'renting'. 'Location de vélo', for instance, means renting a bicycle!

Another interesting example, between Spanish and English, is the word 'REAL'. In English, of course, the word means 'genuine'. As in, 'It is a real diamond.' But in Spanish, the word 'real' actually means 'royal'. So, the king and queen of Spain belong to the 'familia real'.

Finally, we have an example from Hindi and Marathi. Both these languages have the same word, 'KUNDI'. But the word means two very different things in different languages. In Hindi, it means a 'latch'. In Marathi, it means a 'flowerpot'. Can you imagine the confusion if a Hindi-speaker was looking for a latch for their front-door in Pune and was handed a flowerpot?

Can you think of any other such words that you know in languages you speak?

_____
_____
_____
_____

How to Tackle False Cognates?

How do you keep these words separate when you learn them? It can be very easy to confuse false cognates and use them wrongly. To avoid making this mistake, make sure that when you learn the different meanings of the word, you immediately flag this to your brain in a dramatic manner. You can even start by just telling yourself, 'How strange! This word is completely different from the word in the other language!'

If the language spoken has a strongly different accent from yours, you can say that word out loud several times in that accent, emphasizing the difference. Read texts where the word is used and read out the whole text, focusing on the use of that word, so that you understand and store its meaning.

As in the example from Hindi and Marathi, you can also make up imaginary situations where the different uses could lead to funny and complicated situations. This strategy will be extremely effective in groups. For example, can you imagine situations where the word 'REAL' could lead to confusing scenarios between English and Spanish speakers?

Finally, as we suggested for other new words, use them in sentences of your own. And try and make these sentences as dramatic as possible, so that the other meaning registers strongly. They can be as silly as you like, but they have to stand out. You can then mix these up with the other strategies like writing out the word and its meanings in fancy fonts, writing out the sentences that you make up, etc.

SIX

Techniques for Revision and Practice

Since we have looked at techniques to learn new aspects of a language, we will now look at techniques used to revise material you've already learnt, which in turn will boost retention.

Here is a quick recap of all that we have looked at so far:

- Speaking and listening are essential. Unless you hear the right sounds, you will not be able to pronounce words correctly in a language.
- Use as many *authentic* sources as possible to practise listening to and reproducing sounds. This includes:
    - Listening to news broadcasts and radio shows in that language;
    - Watching films and TV shows in that language;
    - Listening to music in that language;
    - Listening closely to native speakers communicate in that language.
- When you are practising how to speak, exaggerate the sounds. That way, you are teaching your mouth what positions to take.
- Reading helps build language skills by teaching you how to form sentences correctly.
- Again, use authentic sources, so that you are reading

language that is approved and correct.
- Read newspapers and magazines, preferably weeklies on current affairs;
- Read comic books (they are a great source of vocabulary and context-based learning);
- Read online articles and even product descriptions;
- Read short stories and novels;
- Read subtitles. Watch your favourite movies with subtitles in the language you want to learn/improve;
- Read road signs and billboards.
- Finally, remember that writing is very important and helps you recall words and spellings much longer than any other type of production.
  - Write letters over and over again. Associate the sounds with other sounds you know;
  - Write as many words as you can in the new language;
  - If you are learning new words, write them out a few times and then write sentences using the words;
  - Use bright colours and fancy fonts to make the words more memorable and also to make learning fun.

All these were tips to use the first time you encountered some new information. In this chapter, we will tell what to do once this information has already been stored your mind. That is, we will tell you how to revise this information so that you will be less likely to forget.

Forgetting + Cycles of Learning

Remember that forgetting is a part of learning as well. By forgetting, your brain either decides that the information is not worth learning after all, and lets it fade away, *or* it indicates that you need to go over the information once more, learning it better or differently.

It forces you to take a look at the strategies you are using to learn. This cycle of relearning will ultimately serve to reinforce the concept. It may take some time and, you may even think to yourself, 'What's that word I keep forgetting, again?' This can be frustrating, but it is a normal part of learning and everyone goes through it.

What this tells us is that there are no *hacks* to learning. There are techniques, which are scientifically studied and proven. Memorizing lists and cramming material may seem to work in the short term, but in the long run, there are more efficient ways to learn.

There is no consensus on exactly why we forget information, but most agree that the mind needs reinforcement at periodic intervals. Here are some theories on why we forget:[14]

- **Cue-dependent forgetting**: Forgetting happens when information has been wrongly encoded. This means that it may be somewhere in our memory, but the mind doesn't have the right retrieval cues or trigger information to fish out the information. This is kind of like hunting for a book in the library without knowing the reference number.

---

[14]Ellis, H.C. and Hunt, R.R., *Fundamentals of Cognitive Psychology* (7th Ed.), Tata McGraw-Hill Publishing Company Limited, New Delhi, 2004.

Byrne, J.H. and Menzel, R. (eds.) 'Learning and Memory: A Comprehensive Reference', *Cognitive Psychology of Memory*, Vol. 2. Academic Press, 2008.

Byrne, J.H. (Ed. in Chief), *Learning and Memory* (2nd Ed.), Thomson Gale, New York, 2017.

- **Interference:** When the mind encounters new information, it competes with existing information, which may then get mixed up and confused, and this ultimately, results in distorted memories. Sometimes, this can happen when we are shifting between two languages. Have you noticed that you start your sentence in one language but a few words from another language creep in?

Knowing this helps you avoid overloading the brain with excess information. For example, while cramming at the last minute, you may find that you mix up two concepts.

Suppose you were learning English and memorizing the following alphabetically arranged list of words, and their meanings:

Baby	Back
Bad	Bag
Ball	Bank
Bar	Base

Try this yourself.

All these *B* words are going to get mixed up in your head. If someone shows you a picture of a bag, you might say it is a ball or a bank. This may happen with other similar sets of information.

This may also be why, when you are trying to answer a question in an exam, you can remember what the page looked like, which part of the book it was in, maybe even the picture next to it but not quite the information you are looking for. This is because all this other information has competed with what you were actually supposed to learn, or it has been encoded in the brain without the correct signals to be able to retrieve it.

Therefore, it got mixed up and your brain doesn't know how to look for the correct information.

Cycles of Learning

Research (as will be demonstrated by the Ebbinghaus curve below) has shown that we need to revise information within specific timelines to be able to store it well.

Here are three numbers for you: 24, 72, 5, 104. Without any reference to what they are, or why you are learning them, it may be a bit difficult.

However, here is some context. A German psychologist called Herman Ebbinghaus plotted a curve that showed that new material you learn is usually forgotten within **twenty-four** hours, unless it is reviewed in this period.

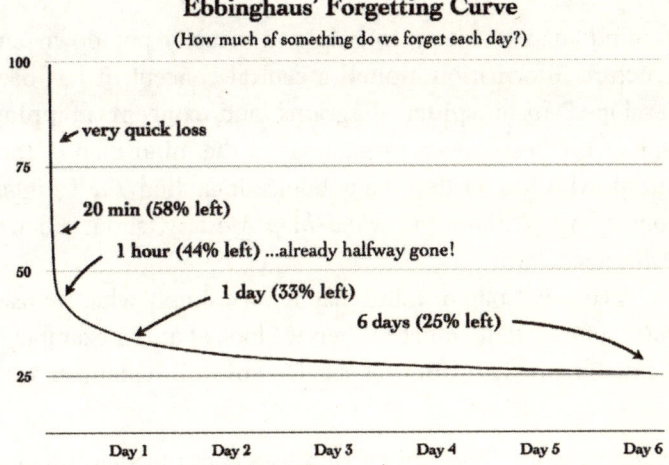

Source: WikimediaCommons/Ebbinghaus curve

Other researchers suggest that this material must be further reviewed again in seventy-two hours and within the week for optimal retrieval. As can be seen in the Ebbinghaus curve, the forgetting or decay slows down over time. That is, there is a sudden fall in the curve (the very quick initial forgetting), but it then levels out and becomes steadier.

This is interpreted as: once you have reviewed the material a few times over the twenty-four hour, seventy-two hour and one-week period, it stays longer and decays more slowly.

This is why we keep emphasizing on creating strong associations, so that the mind can easily retrieve information when needed. This also explains why we need to regularly reinforce information—so that any new information that has come in does not displace it or get wrongly associated and the right associations are strengthened.

Here are some techniques to help you revise information:

Mind Maps

A mind map is a way to help you visually put down and structure information around a central concept. It has been developed from **spider diagrams** and **concept mapping**. One of the best-known proponents of the mind map is Tony Buzan, who has written many books, including *The Ultimate Book of Mind Maps* and *Mind Map Mastery*, about efficient techniques. [15]

A concept map or mind map is very simply what we used in Chapter 3. Remember? When we looked at the example of the dialling code for Bengaluru? Do you still remember what

---

[15] Buzan, Tony, *The Ultimate Book of Mind Maps*, Harper Thorsons, UK, 2012.
——— *Mind Map Mastery: The Complete Guide to Learning and Using the Most Powerful Thinking Tool in the Universe*, Watkins Publishing, 2018.

that number was?

If you do, then you already know about these diagrams. You take a central concept and then just note down all the information you can about it. You can then add more detail to each specific piece of information. Check out the example below. Meghna has taken just a single word, 'walk', and put down as many associations with it as possible. These include how to use the word in various tenses, in different idioms and even its synonyms. She's also included an image to remind herself of the action.

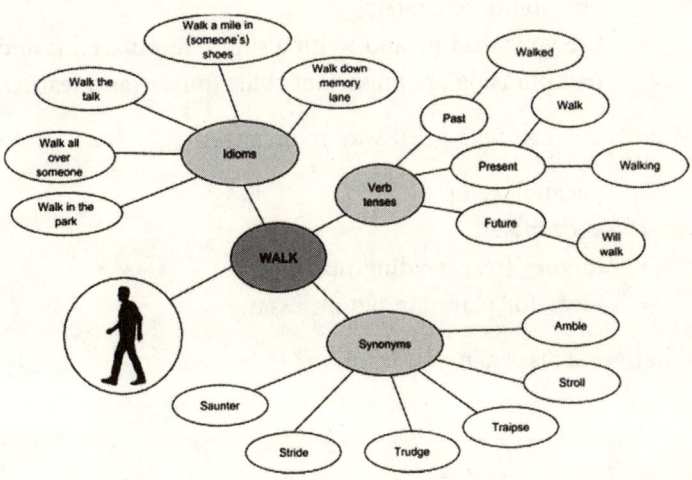

As you can see from the picture, there is a **central concept**—the verb 'walk'. Information is then filed under different **categories**. And each of these, in turn, has further **subdivisions**.

A diagram, like this, can be as plain or as colourful and elaborate as you want. Add symbols and diagrams, highlight keywords, or use different fonts. As we have seen in the previous chapter, how you present information affects how well you learn it. Use information you will remember—for example, your favourite designs or abbreviations. Don't worry about what other people might or might not understand.

A mind map is an excellent technique, because it allows you to:

- consolidate information and concepts;
- put down a good overview of the matter at hand;
- connect ideas in your mind, and form not just mental associations but physical ones on paper;
- process the information for yourself, and not copy out points separately;
- use your reading and writing skills. Summarizing and paraphrasing are important skills to have as a learner.

Mind maps can be a great way to arrange:

- vocabulary lists;
- verb tables;
- themes from reading material;
- ideas for planning out an essay.

What other uses can you think of?

_____

_____

_____

Flashcards

A flashcard is a notecard that has some information on it—words, images and numbers.

Do you remember the pictures of fruits and vegetables your teachers showed you in kindergarten? They can be as simple (but powerful) as that.

It is a great tool to learn and reinforce anything you want

to learn. You could:

- try matching them manually, pair by pair. For example, if you are learning the names of vegetables, you could have pictures of them on some cards and the names on others and you then have to match them correctly;
- hold up a card, and read it out/guess its meaning or sound;
- have a friend show you a card and ask questions about it;
- place cards on a surface to string them together into sentences or categories. These could be cards with words to arrange in the right order, or cards with pictures arranged in an order, which you then have to describe or weave into a story.

Here is an example of flashcards being used to learn vocabulary.

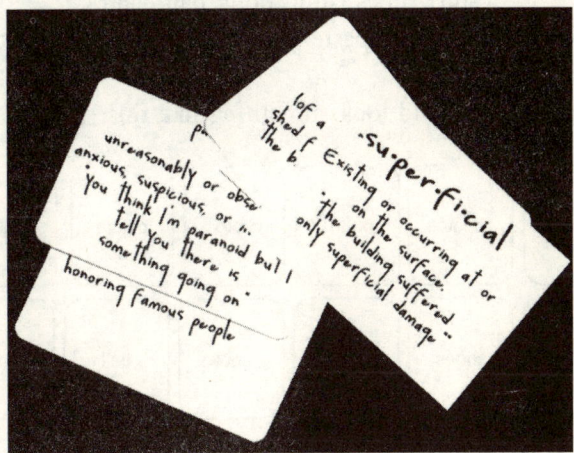

Source: Creative Commons/A. Hallur. From https://flic.kr/p/md3PCV via www.gobloggingtips.com (accessed in 2018)

Flashcards can be made manually using cards or cut up pieces of paper, or using a software on the computer or the phone. Some applications even have pre-made decks of cards.

Of course, making them manually helps reinforce the information. But you can use software and online tools to add images and fancy fonts.

Let us look at two specific exercises to demonstrate how you can use flashcards.

Vocabulary Learning

Method 1: Card Matching

You want to learn the following list of Spanish words:

camisa zapatos nube libro pelota silla

Write each word on an individual flashcard.

Next, write the corresponding English meanings on different flashcards.

shirt shoes cloud book ball chair

Alternatively, draw/paste a picture of each word onto the flashcards.

Your deck would look something like this:

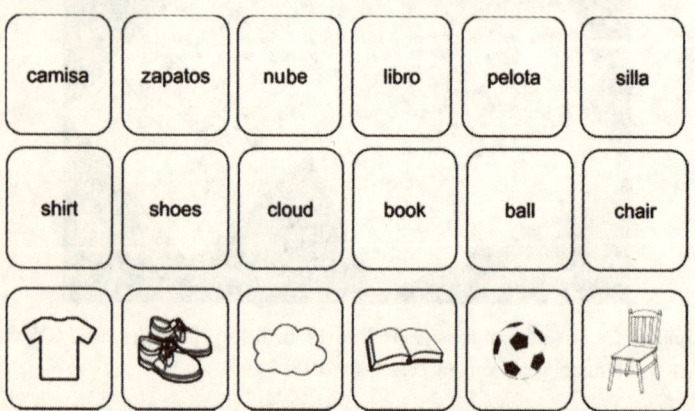

Now, mix up all the cards.

One by one, pick a card. Say the word aloud.

- If you get a picture card, identify it in both Spanish and English.
- If you get a Spanish card, recall the corresponding English word.
- If you get an English card, guess the corresponding Spanish word.

Once you get through all the cards, you will have gone through all the words two or even three times. This is a great way to learn a long list of words. You could even write down the pronunciations or meanings on a set of cards for words that are slightly more challenging or complicated.

Method 2: Memory Game

Let's assume we have the same cards. Take only the Spanish words and the pictures.

Lay them all on a flat surface, with the information (words or pictures) facing down, so you don't know what is on each card.

Now, turn one card over, then turn another. Do they match? If not, turn them both back down and turn the cards over. The first few times you are merely discovering where the different cards are.

But after a few tries, you know the positions of some of the cards.

Let us imagine that the first two cards you turn over are 'camisa' and the picture of the football. They don't match, so you turn them both and choose two other cards at random. At the third try, you turn over a card and it has the word 'pelota' on it. Now, you already know the matching picture that corresponds to this (ball), since you found it at the first attempt. Now, you have to remember where that card was and turn it over. Hey presto! You have a set! Continue in this way and make matching sets for all the words and pictures.

Script Learning

Flashcards can be used to learn scripts as well. In Chapter 5, we studied how we can learn the sounds that correspond to scripts by writing them down as it is pronounced in a language that we are already familiar with. Akhila gave us the example of learning to pronounce the French alphabet by writing the sounds in Tamil and Hindi.

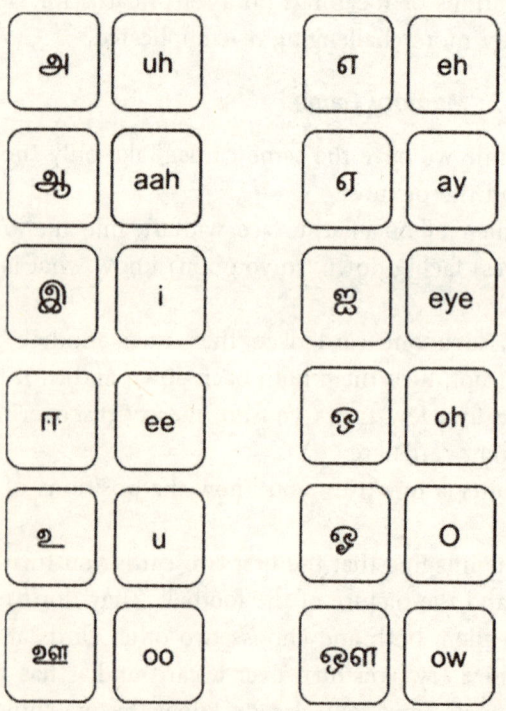

Using the same principle, here is a sample deck of flashcards for Tamil vowels with English pronunciations. Why don't you make similar flashcards and see how quickly you can learn and match the pronunciations by card-matching or through a memory game?

Sentence Structuring/Grammar

Flashcards can be very useful when practising how to write sentences. Often, the order of words in a sentence may vary across languages, and may be a bit confusing. Indian languages differ in this aspect from English.

This is how you would do it.

Write each word/chunk (remember what we said about how to chunk sentences in Chapter 4?) of these sentences onto cards (one chunk per card):

I am going to play in the playground.
She went to write an exam yesterday.
We go to the beach often.
They will be visiting their relatives next week.
He kept the towel in the kitchen.

You can now mix up the cards and then try and find the ones that will fit into a right sentence. You can change the rules slightly to be able to play around with tenses. You can have several different orders:

For example: I go to the playground.
                    She went to the kitchen.

These sentences are only examples. It gives you an idea of the different parts it takes to make up a basic sentence—nouns, verbs, prepositions, articles, adjectives.

Using the cards, see how many combinations of sentences you can make. Remember, you cannot always combine these elements into grammatically correct sentences, as some orders will not be possible. If you are in doubt, check with a friend or anyone you know who speaks the language.

Categories to Learn Vocabulary

One of the best ways of learning vocabulary is to link information with a theme.

Using the methods described above, make a deck of cards with sets of words around different themes or categories. Some examples of possible decks are animals, household items, modes of transport, emotions, days of the week, etc.

Shuffle them all up, and try and group them by category. Read out each word as you pick it up.

Spaced Repetition

In the section on Forgetting, you will remember we said that information needs to be stored correctly, as well as be regularly reinforced.

As can be seen from the Ebbinghaus curve and other research on Ebbinghaus' theory, there is a window of time within which information can be easily forgotten and must be reinforced. Spaced repetition is a technique that utilizes this principle to help you regularly reinforce information at the appropriate intervals.[16]

While the Ebbinghaus curve is a good indicator, you may

---

[16] Ellis, H.C. and Hunt, R.R., *Fundamentals of Cognitive Psychology* (7th Ed.), Tata McGraw-Hill Publishing Company Limited, New Delhi, 2004.

Byrne, J.H. and Menzel, R. (eds.), 'Learning and Memory: A Comprehensive Reference,' *Cognitive Psychology of Memory*, Vol. 2, Academic Press, 2008.

Byrne J.H., (Ed. in Chief), *Learning and Memory* (2nd Ed.), Thomson Gale, New York, 2017.

find that, personally, you retain information longer or for a shorter time. Observe your own learning patterns and what the ideal window for review is for you. By observing how fast you seem to forget what you have learnt, you can form an accurate picture of how often you need to go over the information again. There are several apps and programmes that will test you at appropriate and scientifically determined intervals for maximum retention.

Vocabulary Lists

In Chapter 4, we briefly mentioned the use of vocabulary lists. We have stressed often that rote memorization of these lists is ineffective in the long run. Nevertheless, these lists are good places to start learning vocabulary in a language.

According to some estimates, the first 2,000 words (that is, the most frequently used 2,000 words) in a language make up about 90 per cent of conversation.[17] Just imagine—English is a language of over 1,70,000 words; you need to know just over 1 per cent of these to be conversationally proficient. That makes it seem easy, doesn't it!

There are several lists you can find online for the most common words in any language. These lists are a great place to start. For more complex words in English, try and look out for Scholastic Aptitude Test (SAT) lists.

Another great way to store new words and phrases you come across is to make your own personal dictionary. Or, if you are in the habit of keeping a personal journal/diary, jot down the new words you picked up during the day, along with their meaning, and a practice sentence or two, perhaps?

---

[17]Gardner D., *Exploring Vocabulary. Language in Action*, Routledge, New York, 2013.

You could also type them up somewhere, or bookmark the page you found them on—if it is a web page, or even in an actual book. They may be rare words but try and use these in sentences as often as you can.

Whenever you go back to your physical or online notebook to write in a new word, flip through the older words, even casually, and see if you can remember four or five at random. This will offer simple reinforcement for the other words as well.

Slowly, you will see that you have built up quite the personal lexicon.

Here are some examples from Meghna's personal dictionary for English:

> epicaricacy weltschmerz perspicacity milquetoast
> Pecksniffian sesquipedalian

How many of these did you know? Look them up if you want.

Write some of the new words you have come across recently that you would like to remember.

_____

_____

Worksheet 1

1. Here is an extract from *The Adventures of Sherlock Holmes (Adventure II: The Red-Headed League)* by Sir Arthur Conan Doyle.[18]

   The portly client puffed out his chest with an appearance of some little pride and pulled a dirty and wrinkled

---

[18]Doyle, A.C., *The Adventures of Sherlock Holmes*, Project Gutenberg, Urbana, IL, 2011. Retrieved 5 May 2018, from https://www.gutenberg.org/ebooks/1661

newspaper from the inside pocket of his greatcoat. As he glanced down the advertisement column, with his head thrust forward and the paper flattened out upon his knee, I [John Watson] took a good look at the man and endeavored, after the fashion of my companion, to read the indications which might be presented by his dress or appearance.

I did not gain very much, however, by my inspection. Our visitor bore every mark of being an average commonplace British tradesman, obese, pompous, and slow. He wore rather baggy grey shepherd's check trousers, a not over-clean black frock-coat, unbuttoned in the front, and a drab waistcoat with a heavy brassy Albert chain, and a square pierced bit of metal dangling down as an ornament. A frayed top-hat and a faded brown overcoat with a wrinkled velvet collar lay upon a chair beside him. Altogether, look as I would, there was nothing remarkable about the man save his blazing red head, and the expression of extreme chagrin and discontent upon his features.

Sherlock Holmes' quick eye took in my occupation, and he shook his head with a smile as he noticed my questioning glances. 'Beyond the obvious facts that he has at some time done manual labour, that he takes snuff, that he is a Freemason, that he has been in China, and that he has done a considerable amount of writing lately, I can deduce nothing else.'

Mr. Jabez Wilson started up in his chair, with his forefinger upon the paper, but his eyes upon my companion.

'How, in the name of good-fortune, did you know all that, Mr Holmes?' he asked. 'How did you know, for example, that I did manual labour. It's as true as gospel, for I began as a ship's carpenter.'

'Your hands, my dear sir. Your right hand is quite a size larger than your left. You have worked with it, and the muscles are more developed.'

'Well, the snuff, then, and the Freemasonry?'

'I won't insult your intelligence by telling you how I read that, especially as, rather against the strict rules of your order, you use an arc-and-compass breastpin.'

'Ah, of course, I forgot that. But the writing?'

'What else can be indicated by that right cuff so very shiny for five inches, and the left one with the smooth patch near the elbow where you rest it upon the desk?'

'Well, but China?'

'The fish that you have tattooed immediately above your right wrist could only have been done in China. I have made a small study of tattoo marks and have even contributed to the literature of the subject. That trick of staining the fishes' scales of a delicate pink is quite peculiar to China. When, in addition, I see a Chinese coin hanging from your watch-chain, the matter becomes even more simple.'

Mr Jabez Wilson laughed heavily. 'Well, I never!' said he. 'I thought at first that you had done something clever, but I see that there was nothing in it after all.'

I'm sure you can see from the passage why Sherlock Holmes's deductions are, indeed, legendary. Holmes's skill comes from his ability to make quick associations to information stored in his vast memory. He was a voracious reader and a keen observer of human behaviour.

(a) Now, let's see if you can answer some questions based on the extract in your own words.
   (i) Can you describe some of the things Mr Holmes's guest was wearing?

   _____
   _____

   (ii) What led Mr Holmes to deduce that Mr Wilson had done manual labour in the recent past?

   _____
   _____

   (iii) What was Mr Watson's first impression of the man?

   _____
   _____

   (iv) Only one particular part of Mr Wilson's right cuff was shiny. What did Mr Holmes deduce from this?

   _____
   _____

(b) Are there any words that you didn't know the meaning of? Write them down here. Don't forget to look up the meanings.

   _____
   _____

(c) Do you think you could make deductions like these? Test yourself and your vocabulary to see if you could describe and deduce something about someone. The trick is to have a keen eye, and be able to associate information.

2. Mind mapping can be used effectively to revise material and organize your thoughts.

   Here is an extract from *The Arawack Language of Guiana*

in its Linguistic and Ethnological Relations by D.G. Brinton, 1871.[19]

The Arawacks are a tribe of Indians who at present dwell in British and Dutch Guiana, between the Corentyn and Pomeroon rivers. They call themselves simply lukkunu, men, and only their neighbors apply to them the contemptuous name aruac (corrupted by Europeans into Aroaquis, Arawaaks, Aroacos, Arawacks, etc.), meal-eaters, from their peaceful habit of gaining an important article of diet from the amylaceous pith of the Mauritia flexuosa palm, and the edible root of the cassava plant.

They number only about two thousand souls, and may seem to claim no more attention at the hands of the ethnologist than any other obscure Indian tribe. But if it can be shown that in former centuries they occupied the whole of the West Indian archipelago to within a few miles of the shore of the northern continent, then on the question whether their affiliations are with the tribes of the northern or southern mainland, depends our opinion of the course of migration of the primitive inhabitants of the western world. And if this is the tribe whose charming simplicity Columbus and Peter Martyr described in such poetic language, then the historian will acknowledge a desire to acquaint himself more closely with its past and its present. It is my intention to show that such was their former geographical position.

While in general features, there is nothing to distinguish them from the red race elsewhere, they

---

[19]Brinton, D.G., *The Arawack Language of Guiana in its Linguistic and Ethnological Relations*, Project Gutenberg, Urbana, IL, 2010. Retrieved 14 May 2018, from https://www.gutenberg.org/ebooks/31273.

have strong national traits. Physically they are rather undersized, averaging not over five feet four inches in height, but strong-limbed, agile, and symmetrical. Their foreheads are low, their noses more allied to the Aryan types than usual with their race, and their skulls of that form defined by craniologists as orthognathic brachycephalic.

From the earliest times they have borne an excellent character. Hospitable, peace-loving, quick to accept the humbler arts of civilization and the simpler precepts of Christianity, they have ever offered a strong contrast to their neighbors, the cruel and warlike Caribs. They are not at all prone to steal, lie, or drink, and their worst faults are an addiction to blood-revenge, and a superstitious veneration for their priests.

Why don't you spend five minutes and try and make a quick mind map covering the key points in the passage above about the Arawack tribe. It doesn't have to be very detailed; make sure to put down keywords and phrases only.

If you don't know some of the words, don't forget to look them up!
(Hint: You could categorize it into location, physical traits, character, etc.)

3. Here is a table with the Modern Greek alphabet. Most of the sounds in Greek correspond to those in English.

Upper case	Lower case	Pronunciation in English	Letter sound
A	α	ahl-fa	ah
B	β	vee-tha	between b and v
Γ	γ	gah-ma	between g and h

Upper case	Lower case	Pronunciation in English	Letter sound
Δ	δ	del-tha	d as in 'this'
E	ε	ehp-sil-on	eh
Z	ζ	zee-tha	z
H	η	ee-tha	ee
Θ	θ	thee-tha	th
I	ι	yo-tha	ee
K	κ	kah-pa	k
Λ	λ	lamb-da	l
M	μ	mi	m
N	ν	ni	n
Ξ	ξ	ksee	k
O	o	oh-mi-kron	oh
Π	π	pi	p
P	ρ	rroh	rr
Σ	σ ς	sig-ma	s
T	τ	tahf	th
Υ	υ	ip-sil-on	i
Φ	φ	fee	f
*X	χ	hee	~h as in 'loch' or 'Khan'
Ψ	ψ	psee	s
Ω	ω	oh-meh-ga	oh

*Those marked with an asterisk do not have an exactly corresponding Indian–English pronunciation.

You may recognize some alphabets from lessons at school—this is because many of the natural sciences use Greek alphabets in calculations and formulae to denote certain agreed-upon units and measures. For example, the letter λ can refer to wavelength of electromagnetic radiation, Ω to electrical resistance and ρ to density. However, some of the pronunciations you have learnt for the alphabets are anglicized. The table has the pronunciations from modern Greek.

Study the table of alphabets. If you have paper handy, make a deck of flashcards. Each card must have either an alphabet or its pronunciation. Feel free to write down the pronunciation of the alphabet in a language of your choosing.

Practise your Greek alphabet using your flashcards by playing the memory game that was described earlier.

Games for Groups

All these are very common games and you must have played them in different contexts. But we specify here how you can adapt them easily to the language context to fix new vocabulary and attach greater meaning to it! The game is for two to six people.

The first one is simply called **Categories**. People sit in a group and then start clapping. We have indicated what each player says and, within brackets, we have indicated the action that follows whatever they say. All the words and spoken statements must fit into the two beats between claps. The game follows the below rhythms:

Player 1: Categories (everyone claps twice)
Player 2: Will you please (everyone claps twice)
Player 3: Name some (everyone claps twice) names of (everyone claps twice)
Player 4: ANIMALS (everyone claps twice). [This player can call out any category they wish: plants, animals, birds, cars, family members, etc.]

Player 5: Zebra (everyone claps twice)
Player 6: Buffalo (everyone claps twice)

And so on... However, if anyone repeats a word that has already been used by another player for that category, they are 'out' and the game continues with the remaining players.

If a player cannot think of anything, he/she can ask for 'Change please' quickly, within two claps.

All the answers have to fit the interval between two claps. So, a player will get out if they:

(1) repeat an answer that has been used in that category;
(2) cannot say anything between two claps;
(3) forget to clap.

This is a fun game and a great way to learn vocabulary in different domains. You could use it to learn the names of vegetables or rooms in a house or classroom objects!

You could even add your own twist to it, where people switch between different languages. Ensure that all players follow the same set of languages.

The second game is **Antakshari**. Many of you are sure to be familiar with this game. Each player has to give an answer beginning with the last sound/syllable of the previous answer. A group can play this without sticking to categories just to revise vocabulary.

For example: In an English class:

Student 1: Newspaper
Student 2: Raincoat
Student 3: Tamarind
Student 4: Dalmation

And so on...

Here you can tweak the game in your group. You can make it either the last letter (for example, if someone says 'Checkmate', then the next person begins with 'E', instead of the 'T' sound) or the last sound (with 'Checkmate', the next person would begin with the 'T' sound in 'Checkmate') or any other twist you can come up with.

Perhaps you could time it. Or, decide to stick to a theme. Whatever you choose, this is a good way of bonding and helping each other recall words you have come across.

Incremental Games are another great way to encourage learning in a group. There are two types of games in this category. One involves simply naming objects and using basic sentences. The other involves complex sentences and storytelling.

Listing: This game can be used to revise specific objects by creating a 'list' that students have to remember and add to.

For example, if the topic was 'clothes and accessories', the game could be as follows.

Student 1: I am going on vacation and I am packing in one pink t-shirt.

Student 2: I am going on vacation and I am packing in one pink t-shirt and one red scarf.

Student 3: I am going on vacation and I am packing in one pink t-shirt, one red scarf and one pair of green socks...

In this way, each student repeats the original sentence, lists and adds one item to it.

This is a great way to learn to use simple sentences ('I am going on vacation...') and revise objects and descriptions ('one red scarf, an old hat...').

Story Building: This game is again one that many people might be familiar with. It involves creating a story together, with each person adding their plot to the story. This is a fun game because nobody knows what each person will add and the person after them has to try and put in some context or explanation.

A very quick example of this:

Student 1: Once upon a time, in a very large castle on the banks of a river, there lived a princess...

Student 2: ... The princess was an old lady of eighty-four, loved swimming in the river and talking to the birds, and hated people. However...

Student 3: ...the only person she did not hate was the little girl who rowed her across the river every day for a swim. This girl was...

Student 4: ...actually the daughter of a wicked witch, but nobody knew this! The witch wanted the old princess' crown and jewels and so...

Student 5: ...she hid behind a tree and whenever the princess went out for a swim, she would sneak into the palace disguised as the princess and steal one jewel!

As you can see, each person can add anything that they wish to. Someone could even introduce a spaceship or time travel!

A few rules would make this easier—each student must give one or two lines of the story, end in the middle of a sentence and then the next person must complete the last line. Also, you can set a limit on how long the story should be and how long each person can take to complete it.

Of course, all our examples here are in English, just to

make it convenient for us and for you to understand the games. However, these can be played using any language. English, Hindi, French, Czech, Swahili—the same games can be used in multiple languages and with any number of variations to build fluency and to help you recall vocabulary and to use it correctly.

In two of the worksheets at the end of the book, we have given you **story prompts** to help you do this yourself through writing or talking aloud. You can find more such prompts on the Internet—they're great for working with any language.

Conclusion

So, here we are! It seems fitting that at the end of a book on memory, we are going to recall all that we learnt.

Right after this summary, we have a set of worksheets that will help you recall everything we are speaking about here. So, don't worry if something seems strange or you think you still haven't understood some techniques.

In Chapter 1, we examined popular ideas around memory and also looked at two theories. One theory said that we pay attention to something, then **rehearse** it and it then gets stored in our **long-term memory**.

Another theory said that how information is stored depends on how much **processing** is carried out, as the greater the meaning, the better the remembering.

In Chapter 2, we looked at how people acquire languages. All humans are born almost pre-programmed to learn languages. Right from when we're born, we start paying attention to sounds and by the time we're a few months old, we are able to start telling sounds apart and producing them ourselves. By the time we're two, we can use short words together. And by the time we're four or five, we're using many words, building proper sentences, and understanding and sharing stories.

Our vocabulary continues to grow throughout our life, though most of our understanding of grammar and language rules is acquired in childhood.

We can also learn new languages throughout our life—

though this learning is not as natural as with our first language and we need to put in more time and effort into learning words and understanding how to put them together correctly.

In Chapter 3, we discussed different memory techniques.

Chapter 4 examined the first skills any human develops in language: listening and speaking.

The key strategies covered here included:

- Exaggerated pronunciation;
- Repetition;
- Listening to a variety of audio and watching videos;
- Roleplaying.

Chapter 5 looked at skills that need to be learnt in *any* language, even our first language: reading and writing.

It looked at the difficulties that these skills pose and why it takes children longer to learn to write and read than to speak. It then covered a few simple strategies to enhance our memory and for learning a language through reading and writing. It also threw light on the use of various techniques while reading and writing to improve your language skills and remember important words and grammar rules.

- Reading aloud;
- Reading a variety of texts;
- Summarizing what you read;
- Writing down meanings;
- Repetitive actions;
- Using fancy fonts and bright colours.

Finally, Chapter 6 examined strategies you can use for **revising** information that you have already learnt using the information from earlier chapters. The chief strategies covered here were:

- Flashcards;
- Mind maps;
- Elaborative rehearsal;
- Games for groups.

There was a lot of information in this book—perhaps too much to take in at once. But in order to demonstrate the practical application of everything that we have discussed, we now have a set of worksheets for you to try.

We recommend that you have the following materials ready:

- Pencils (plain or colour);
- Pens (plain or colour);
- Blank sheets or a notebook;
- Cards for flashcards (you can also just cut plain paper into small squares or rectangles).

And there you go! That's all you need to practice to effectively learn and remember a new language.

We hope that through this book and all the activities in the worksheets that follow, you are able to understand how your brain responds to information:

- Some people seem to respond better to pictures and stories;
- Some people respond better to reading and taking precise notes;
- Some people learn more from carrying out actions.

Pay attention to all the activities on the worksheet. Which one(s) do you find the most helpful? Once you identify that, you can then use these strategies for learning any material (not only for languages).

We also strongly encourage you to take these tips and modify them for yourself. Or even come up with new ones!

All this time, we've talked about how a good memory can improve your language skills, but did it ever occur to you that learning languages, in turn, can improve your memory?

Keeping your mind sharp and in good condition is all about challenging yourself constantly and using it regularly. A great way to challenge yourself using language is **word games**.

Word games are those that use your knowledge of language in the game. These can be played alone, like Crosswords or word searches. You can also play with other people, as in Scrabble, Boggle or Pictionary. They can be a fun way to challenge yourself, *and* keep your mind sharp!

Learning resources on the Internet

Here are some useful links and resources to help you along the way:

For those interested in learning new languages, Duolingo and Memrise are good platforms to get started.

To practise your pronunciations, visit the website Forvo. It contains a crowdsourced database of pronunciations for practically every word in every popular language. Even you can contribute to it! If you want to hear what different accents of the world sound like, head to Localingual!

Some great flashcard apps include Anki, Mnemosyne and Quizlet. They let you make your own decks, and provide you with timely reminders for practice to maintain maximum retention. They vary in complexity of use, so why not try them all and see which one works for you?

For fun language learning games, go to Digital Dialects, which has games in more than forty different languages!

For those interested in the different languages of the world, visit Ethnologue and Omniglot—they are encyclopediae of different languages. They tell you about the language, where it is spoken, the basic sounds, the alphabet, etc. It is, indeed, a fun way to learn about the world.

And finally, for those interested in language itself, perhaps Linguistics is for you. There are plenty of resources on the Internet to start exploring this field. Try learning the IPA as well.

Worksheets

In some exercises in these worksheets, we have decided to use languages and scripts that are more likely to be unfamiliar to readers, though some of them you may already know. If this is the case, we suggest that you look up some languages and scripts that you don't know and then follow those particular exercises, as they are meant to show you how to approach new information and process it.

We have also stuck to using *left-to-right* scripts, and avoided pictographic and logographic scripts (scripts that use images or meaningful symbols to denote words or syllables, like those in many East Asian languages, hieroglyphics, or even emojis). The exercises can be completed in any order.

These worksheets are meant to help the reader apply all of the techniques introduced in the book.

Worksheet 1

1. Using association to learn new scripts

As we have discussed in Chapter 5, one of the biggest challenges in learning new scripts is remembering which sound each letter signifies. One way to **anchor** this is to connect the letters to sounds you already know.

Here is the modern Russian (Cyrillic) alphabet, with both capital and small letters. Many of the alphabets are similar to English but may have a different sound entirely.

Fun fact: Just like English writing can be in print (separate letters) or in cursive (all connected letters), in Russian, there is one series of alphabets for the printed form and another for handwritten (cursive) letters, which allows for speed when writing. The series we have given below is in the print form. If you are interested, you can go on to the handwritten letters, which are easily available on the Internet.

We have given the closest pronunciation in English, corresponding to each alphabet.

Alphabet	English pronunciation	Alphabet	English pronunciation
А а	aah	Р р	err
Б б	beh	С с	es
В в	veh	Т т	theh
Г г	geh	У у	oo
Д д	deh	Ф ф	ef
Е е	yeh	Х х*	~ ha (as in 'loch' or 'eugh' or 'Khan')
Ё ё	yo	Ц ц	tseh
Ж ж	zheh (as in 'pleasure' or 'vision')	Ч ч	cheh
З з	zeh	Ш ш	sha
И и	ee	Щ щ	scha
Й й	ee krath-kuhyuh (stressed ee or 'eeyeh' sound)	Ъ^	the hard sign (no sound)
К к	kah	ы*	~ iy
Л л	el	Ь^	the soft sign (no sound)
М м	em	Э э	eh
Н н	en	Ю ю	yoo
О о	oh	Я я	ya
П п	pueh		

*those marked with an asterisk do not have an exactly corresponding Indian-English pronunciation. Do look them up online on one of the websites we suggested!

^the hard and soft signs do not have any sounds of their own but appear with certain vowels to soften or harden the attached consonants. A consonant is softened when it is palatalized, that is, when it is pronounced with the middle of the tongue raised to the roof of the mouth (palate). The hard sign is used less often, and is used to stress that a consonant must not be palatalized. We, however, do not have to use either for the purpose of our exercises.

(a) Use a combination of the following strategies:
  i) **Exaggerated pronunciations**: Read out the letters slowly and dramatically in order.
  ii) Write down the **letters** in one column and then write down the **sound** of each letter in a non-English language you may know (an Indian language or any other).

Alphabet practice	Pronunciation in your chosen language	Alphabet practice	Pronunciation in your chosen language

  iii) **Chunking:** Group the alphabet in any way you choose—into categories, for example, letters that look similar, or vowels *or* grouping them in some order, as in Hindi 'ka, kha, ga, gha'. Learning the letters in groups will help you remember them.

Based on the alphabet and corresponding sounds given above, if you were to learning the Russian alphabet, how would you group the sounds? How would *you* chunk the Russian alphabet? Write them down here.

After rehearsing this in different ways, practise. Try to write or reproduce any **ten letters** and say the alphabet **aloud**. You could spend half an hour to forty-five minutes or even a few hours on it. There are no extra points for finishing early.

2. (*At least two hours later*) Use the above letters to write simple words in English or any other familiar language, to make sure you remember them. Revise them once (thrice at most!) if you want to be sure.

E.g. The English word 'Marvel' can be written as 'Марвэл'.

We are not going to learn Russian words. You have to write the English words as **pronounced**, using Russian letters—this exercise is only to practise the alphabet!

(a) Here are some English words for you to try:
   i) Goat ——————————————
   ii) Tremble ——————————————
   iii) Drastic ——————————————

(b) Write down three words of your choice here using the Russian alphabet (the word can be from any language you are familiar with)

   ——————————————————————
   ——————————————————————
   ——————————————————————

(c) What aspect of the language do you think this activity tests?

i) Writing;
ii) Letter shape and sound association;
iii) Vocabulary building;
iv) Memory

3. Can you see any similarity between the Russian letters and the script used for your native tongue? Or, Russian sounds and any exact matches in your native tongue? Remember—building associations between what you already know makes new information that much easier to learn.

For example; 'd' in Russian (Д) is like an incomplete 'k' (க) in Tamil. But it is also a little like the written form of the Tamil letter that has the same sound as the Russian letter ('da'). The 'zh' (Ж) in Russian loosely looks like 'झ' in Devnagri, or even simply two conjoined English *K*s.

What are the differences? For example; 'b' is not a 'beh' sound in Russian, but a 'veh' sound.

Write both similarities and differences down here if you can think of any.

_____
_____
_____
_____
_____

4. **Spider Diagram (mind map) Activity**: Vocabulary maps
   Here are two words.

   (a) Red
   (b) Nudge

Now, draw a list of ways in which these words can be used; write down as many expressions as you can find that use the words.

You can refer to the spider diagram for 'Walk' in Chapter 6. The central theme or concept must be in the centre, and spread outward like a spider.

5. Read the following passage two or three times. Ideally read it aloud. Remember to use intonations, emotions and any other techniques you'd like to use for reading aloud.

> Gilbert Blythe was trying to make Anne Shirley look at him and failing utterly, because Anne was at that moment totally **oblivious** not only to the very existence of Gilbert Blythe, but of every other scholar in Avonlea school itself. With her chin **propped** on her hands and her eyes fixed on the blue glimpse of the Lake of Shining Waters that the west window afforded, she was far away in a gorgeous dreamland hearing and seeing nothing save her own wonderful visions.
>
> Gilbert Blythe wasn't used to putting himself out to make a girl look at him and meeting with failure. She should look at him, that red-haired Shirley girl with the little pointed chin and the big eyes that weren't like the eyes of any other girl in Avonlea school.
>
> Gilbert reached across the **aisle**, picked up the end of Anne's long red braid, held it out at arm's length and said in a piercing whisper:
>
> 'Carrots! Carrots!'
>
> Then Anne looked at him with a vengeance!
>
> She did more than look. She sprang to her feet, her bright fancies fallen into **cureless** ruin. She flashed one **indignant** glance at Gilbert from eyes whose angry sparkle was swiftly quenched in equally angry tears.
>
> 'You mean, hateful boy!' she exclaimed passionately. 'How dare you!'

And then—thwack! Anne had brought her slate down on Gilbert's head and cracked it—slate not head—clear across.

Avonlea's school always enjoyed a scene. This was an especially enjoyable one. Everybody said 'Oh' in horrified delight. Diana gasped. Ruby Gillis, who was inclined to be hysterical, began to cry.

The above is an extract from *Anne of Green Gables* by L.M. Montgomery.[20]

Read this again and once you are done, we will come to this in a while.

6. Here's another mind mapping activity:

(a) Find two or three synonyms or explanations, as well as different phrases that use the following simple words and put them in a mind map.

   i) Cat

   ii) Dog

   iii) Jump

---

[20]Montgomery, L.M., *Anne of Green Gables*. Project Gutenberg, Urbana, IL, 2008. Retrieved on June 28, 2018, from http://www.gutenberg.org/ebooks/45

124 • *Fast and Fluent*

(Yes, 'cat' and 'dog' seem very silly words, we know! But do try and look them up in a thesaurus or dictionary—you might be surprised by how differently they can be used in different contexts!)

   (b) Use synonym for these two words in at least one or two new sentences.
      i) Dog

      _____

      _____

      ii) Jump

      _____

      _____

7. Remember the passage about Anne?

   (a) Get ready to answer some questions from the passage:
      i) What does Gilbert whisper in class? What was he referring to?

      _____

      _____

      ii) How does Anne react? What does she hit Gilbert with?

      _____

      _____

   (b) Here are the words that were highlighted:
      Oblivious Propped Aisle Indignant Cureless

        Which of these words were you unfamiliar with? Could you figure out the meaning from context? Look them up if you don't know. Use each of these words in two sentences of your own.
      i) Oblivious

      _____

      _____

ii) Propped

___

iii) Aisle

___

iv) Indignant

___

v) Cureless

___

(c) Why do you think we asked you to come back to it? Could you remember this information, even though some time has passed since you read the passage?

Worksheet 2

1. Word association exercise

An important way to build foundations in a new language is to build *associations*.

When learning vocabulary, a great way to learn new words is by association.

So, for example, take this image:*

Use this as a starting point, and connect words that strike you when you look at this image, with each word building on the previous one.

Here is a series of associations that Meghna made:

Clock → Time → Father → Beard → Hair → Fragrant → Flowery

The sequence of words may not make sense to you, but these are the first words that came to mind for her.

Here's an alternative series of words:

Clock → Hands → To scratch → Itchy → Chicken pox → Sick → Holiday

As you can see, the starting point can be the same (but not necessarily! She could have used 'watch' or 'time' or 'round'), but the mind can make so many connections at once. These can include objects, sensations, actions, emotions—anything.

Now, what if you were to try this in a different language, one that you already know or are learning? You could write down a series directly in that language, or look up new words if you don't already know them.

If Meghna were practising her Spanish, another series would look something like this:

El reloj → Corriendo → El ejercicio → Cansado → Dormir → Contento → La sonrisa
[Clock → Running → Exercise → Tired → To sleep → Happy → Smile]

She didn't know the word for 'tired' and 'clock', so she looked them up. Now, she not only knows two new words, but has made *associations* for these in her mind.

Try this yourself now. For each image, try making **two**

different series of words—one in English, and one in any other language of your choice. If you do not know a particular word, try and look up the translation. If not, see what other connections your mind may make.

Make sure each series has *at least* **five** words. If you want, try and leave a gap of about ten minutes between the series so that your mind is fresh, and the words from the previous attempt don't *interfere* with new ones.

(a)

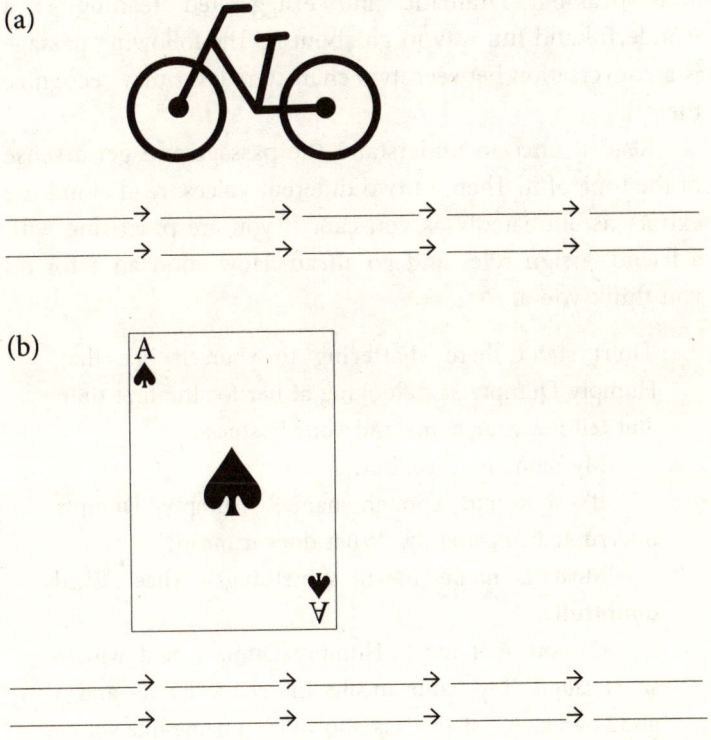

_____ → _____ → _____ → _____ → _____
_____ → _____ → _____ → _____ → _____

(b)

_____ → _____ → _____ → _____ → _____
_____ → _____ → _____ → _____ → _____

(c)

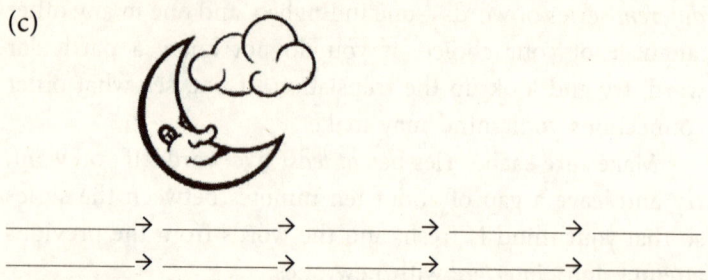

———→ ———→ ———→ ———→ ———
———→ ———→ ———→ ———→ ———

2. In Chapter 4, we spoke about practising your pronunciation and speaking. Dramatic and exaggerated reading is a wonderful and fun way to go about it. The following passage is a conversation between two characters (you may recognize them!).

Read it once to understand the passage and get a sense of the tone of it. Then, in two different voices, read aloud the extract as animatedly as you can. If you are practising with a friend, assign roles and go ahead. How good an actor do you think you are?

> 'Don't stand there **chattering** to yourself like that,' Humpty Dumpty said, looking at her for the first time, 'but tell me your name and your business.'
>
> 'My name is Alice, but…'
>
> 'It's a stupid enough name!' Humpty Dumpty interrupted impatiently. 'What does it mean?'
>
> 'Must a name mean something?' Alice asked **doubtfully**.
>
> 'Of course it must,' Humpty Dumpty said with a short laugh: 'my name means the shape I am—and a good handsome shape it is, too. With a name like yours, you might be any shape, almost.'
>
> 'Why do you sit out here all alone?' said Alice, not

wishing to begin an argument.

'Why, because there's nobody with me!' cried Humpty Dumpty. 'Did you think I didn't know the answer to that? Ask another.'

'Don't you think you'd be safer down on the ground?' Alice went on, not with any idea of making another riddle, but simply in her good-natured **anxiety** for the queer creature. 'That wall is so very narrow!'

'What tremendously easy riddles you ask!' Humpty Dumpty growled out. 'Of course I don't think so! Why, if ever I did fall off—which there's no chance of—but if I did—' Here he pursed his lips and looked so **solemn** and grand that Alice could hardly help laughing. 'If I did fall,' he went on, 'The King has promised me—with his very own mouth—to—to—'

'To send all his horses and all his men,' Alice interrupted, rather unwisely.

'Now I declare that's too bad!' Humpty Dumpty cried, breaking into a sudden passion. 'You've been listening at doors—and behind trees—and down chimneys—or you couldn't have known it!'

'I haven't, indeed!' Alice said very gently. 'It's in a book.'

'Ah, well! They may write such things in a book,' Humpty Dumpty said in a calmer tone. 'That's what you call a History of England, that is. Now, take a good look at me! I'm one that has spoken to a King, I am: mayhap you'll never see such another: and to show you I'm not proud, you may shake hands with me!' And he grinned almost from ear to ear, as he leant forwards (and as nearly as possible fell off the wall in doing so) and offered Alice his hand. She watched him a little anxiously as she took it. 'If he smiled much more, the ends of his mouth might meet behind,' she thought: 'and then I don't know what would happen to his head! I'm afraid it would come off!'

'Yes, all his horses and all his men,' Humpty Dumpty went on. 'They'd pick me up again in a minute, they would! However, this conversation is going on a little too fast: let's go back to the last **remark** but one.'

'I'm afraid I can't quite remember it,' Alice said very politely.

The above is an extract from *Through the Looking-Glass* by Lewis Carroll.[21]

i) How does Alice know what the King promised? Have you heard the name 'Humpty Dumpty' before? Do you remember what happens to Humpty Dumpty after all?

_____

_____

_____

ii) 'What does it [your name] mean?' Humpty Dumpty had asked Alice. His name, he said, described the shape of his body. In India, people are usually given names drawn from words that have meaning in our languages. What does you name mean and what language is it from?

_____

_____

_____

---

[21]Carroll, L., *Through the Looking-Glass*, Project Gutenberg, Urbana, IL, 2011. Retrieved 27 June 2018, from http://www.gutenberg.org/ebooks/12

Find out the meanings of the names of five people you know and translate them into English.

_____

_____

_____

_____

iii) Here are some words from the passage:
Chattering Doubtfully Anxiety Solemn Remark

Create a short story using all of these words. It can be as short as three lines but make sure to use **all** the words, and be as **descriptive** as possible.

_____

_____

_____

3. Do you enjoy riddles? Humpty Dumpty certainly seems to—he thinks every question is a riddle! He is someone who takes everything *literally*. This means following the exact meaning of every word, leaving no room for metaphors, figures of speech or approximations.

All languages have several figures of speech and common metaphors.

For example, in English, the phrase 'to have cold feet' means to not go through with something, usually because one is scared. Or take, 'to let the cat out of the bag'. It doesn't necessarily mean to release a cat from a bag but to reveal some piece of information that wasn't meant to be revealed.

In Spanish, for example, one may say '*Tomar el pelo*' which *literally* translates to 'to take the hair', but *figuratively* means 'to pull one's leg' or 'to joke around with/fool someone'. Similarly, '*Tener un humor de perros*' *literally* means 'to have the mood of dogs' but *figuratively* means 'to be in a bad mood'.

Figures of speech, metaphors and proverbs are commonly used in all languages, and being fluent in a language will mean knowing some basic phrases and idioms. These phrases are also a great way to learn and remember vocabulary, because the imagery is often quite bizarre (creating great associations) and, therefore, powerful!

Can you list five such idioms in English or a language of your choice? Look some up, or ask someone for help if you do not know.

i. _____
ii. _____
iii. _____
iv. _____
v. _____

4. In the same novel (*Through the Looking-Glass*), we come across the characters called Tweedledum and Tweedledee. Here is short poem about them:

Tweedledum and Tweedledee
    Agreed to have a battle;
For Tweedledum said Tweedledee
    Had spoiled his nice new rattle.

Just then flew down a monstrous crow,
    As black as a tar-barrel;
Which frightened both the heroes so,
    They quite forgot their quarrel.

You may not know who Tweedledum and Tweedledee are but the names certainly invoke an image in the mind! Who do you think they are? Do you think they are like Humpty Dumpty?

With a friend or partner, **roleplay** a conversation as

Tweedledum and Tweedledee, quarrelling about something, (perhaps one of you breaking the other's toy). How would you feel? What would make you stop fighting (as the 'monstrous crow' did in the poem)? Remember, try voices and accents to make it stick in the mind. Imagine what the Tweedles are like as people.

Try this in a language that you are learning or want to practise. This exercise will help you recall and express *emotion* words, and improve your fluency.

5. An effective method of learning something is the Method of Loci (Chapters 3 and 4). People have learnt entire novels using just this method. You can read more about them on the Internet.

Someone who has developed the ability to learn large amounts of data is known as a **mnemonist.** Did you know that there are even competitions of memory, like the World Memory Championships and Extreme Memory Tournament? People who participate in this do not have any extraordinary ability but simply employ mnemonic techniques effectively.

Do you think you could be a mnemonist?

Let's see if you can use the Method of Loci to learn the short poem above.

If you recall, you have to imagine a familiar space and all its intricate detail. Next, you are going to place words along a fixed route, say from your room to the hallway. Rehearse this route in your head, and where you put words. As you rehearse, you are going to start associating the sequence of the poem with the route taken.

Instead of putting *every single* word, it is more efficient to place only keywords, leaving out filler words like 'a', 'the', 'of' and so on.

Therefore, in this poem, you might start with:

Tweedledum → Tweedledee → agreed → to have → battle → Tweedledum → said → Tweedledee → spoiled → nice new rattle → and so on.

There! That was already the first stanza!

If you are confident in the use of this method, you could use short forms and drop words you are sure your brain will fill in.

For example, Dum → Dee → agreed → battle → Dum → Dee → spoiled → rattle.

This is much shorter!

Now, follow the same process for stanza two.

Close your eyes and imagine vividly where the words are. After you are done rehearsing, give a gap of ten minutes, close your eyes and try and recite the poem. How well did you do?

Now, try after a gap of a day. Where you able to recall the poem as well?

*Image Credits

Ace of Spades@Openclipart/Casino
Moon-lineart@Openclipart/Frankes
Bicycle Pictogram@Openclipart/Libberry
Clock@Openclipart/palomaironique

Worksheet 3

1. Go back to the Russian alphabet learnt through Worksheet 1. Refer to it for a **maximum** of three minutes before beginning this activity.

    Write out the following English words using

the corresponding sounds in the Russian alphabet. **Approximate** sounds if there is no direct equivalent:
   (a) Book _____
   (b) Unicorns _____
   (c) Procrastinate _____
   (d) Conscience _____
2. Find one synonym for each of the following words:
   (a) Green _____
   (b) Fizzy _____
   (c) Solid _____
   (d) Smiling _____

Now use the Storytelling/Elaborative method (Chapter 5) to make a short story using the synonyms you found in order to remember them. Be as descriptive as you can.

3. Chart out, in the form of a spider diagram, the various uses (phrases and idioms) of the following word. Also, write or draw the meaning of the word.
   WATER
4. Draw a concept map of your favourite book or movie (or the last book or movie you read/watched). Remember to chart out the names of the main character, their principal qualities, how they ended up relating to each other and one or two ideas you took away from the book/movie.

_____
_____
_____
_____
_____
_____

5. Here are the first two stanzas from Lewis Carroll's poem 'Jabberwocky'[22] (which we also read earlier in the book). Can you read it out dramatically? How many lines can you remember after reading it out twice or thrice with expression and gestures?

Twas brillig, and the slithy toves
>Did gyre and gimble in the wabe:

All mimsy were the borogoves,
>And the mome raths outgrabe.

'Beware the Jabberwock, my son!
>The jaws that bite, the claws that catch!

Beware the Jubjub bird, and shun
>The frumious Bandersnatch!'

6. The 'Jabberwocky' poem above is full of nonsense words and may sound like someone speaking with a cold! I can imagine it is a bit hard to remember. But, what it does have, is plenty of rhymes.

    Try setting the first paragraph of the poem to song (or even the second, if you're feeling up to it), just as we talked about in Chapter 4. Give it a catchy tune and repeat it to yourself.

    The best way to know if your song works is to teach it to someone else. Spend no more than **five** minutes teaching someone your new song. How soon did they pick it up?

    Come back to it a week later. Do you still remember your song?

---

[22]Carroll, L., *Through the Looking-Glass*, Project Gutenberg, Urbana, IL, 2011. Retrieved 27 June 2018, from http://www.gutenberg.org/ebooks/12

Worksheet 4

1. English has evolved from multiple languages over the years. It has borrowed and adapted words, even grammar. Some of its biggest influences are Latin, Greek and Germanic languages. Many Indian words have become a part of the English lexicon (as was noted in Chapter 2).

Refer to the table with the Greek alphabet in Chapter 6. The table gives you the approximated English sound for each alphabet. Given that all the Greek words in English have been modified in some way, perhaps we should study some *actual* Greek words.

Here are some basic words in modern Greek. Referring to the alphabet table, see if you can figure out the pronunciation of the word and write it down *in English*. Next, write the pronunciation of this word in another language of your choosing. Remember to also read them out loud—it will help with your pronunciation.

Note: Letters that have the accent on top (ή, ώ, έ) indicate stress on that letter/syllable.

Greek word	Meaning	Pronunciation in English	Pronunciation in other language
Καλημέρα	Good morning		
Ευχαριστώ	Thank you		
Συγνώμη	Excuse me/Sorry		
Βοήθεια	Help!		
Παρακαλώ	Please/You're welcome		

2. When you think of birthdays, one immediately associates things, such as cake, candles, balloons and the birthday song.

These associations have been reinforced time and again over the years every time you go for a birthday party, or see one on television.

We all know the birthday song in English. Did you know that several other languages have their own versions of the song, all set to the same tune?

Here is the Spanish version (with the English translation next to it):

Cumpleaños feliz	Happy birthday
Cumpleaños feliz	Happy birthday
Te deseamos todos	We all wish you
Cumpleaños feliz	Happy birthday

Sing the Spanish version in the same melody as the English one. A technique that will help you here is to break up the words into smaller bits (**chunks**) to fit the rhythm of the song.

Note: The 'ñ' in Spanish has a 'ny' sound, so it is pronounced as 'cum-pleh-ah-nyos'; 't' is pronounced 'th'.

Now, wasn't that simple?

You have also learnt that '*cumpleaños Feliz*' means 'Happy birthday'. You can also deduce the meanings of words from the next line, '*Te deseamos todos*'.

3. (a) While we're talking about birthdays, here is a list of birthday-related words:

Balloon Blow Cake Game
Gift Play Wish Year
Invite Colourful Fun Happy

Using flashcards (or paper you have cut into rectangles), draw the meaning of the words on one set of cards. Next, write the words out in a different language, preferably one you are learning. Feel free to add any related words you can think of, to the set.

Play the Memory Game (from Chapter 6) to learn these new words. You should be able to look at an image and recall the word for it in the language you are learning. Similarly, when presented with a word, you should be able to recall the correct meaning.

(b) Choose **two of the five** categories given. Make flashcards with words written on one set, and drawings on the other.

Characteristics Sea Shopping Holidays Art

Come up with **at least ten** words for each category. These can be descriptive words, actions you do, emotions you feel—anything.

4. An **acrostic** is when the first letter, word or syllable in a line spells out a poem or text. They can help you remember spellings. All you have to do is remember your little poem. They also help improve your writing skills.

Here is an example from *Through the Looking-Glass* by Lewis Carroll (again!). The first letter of every line together spells Alice Pleasance Liddell, the protagonist's full name.

> **A** boat, beneath a sunny sky
> **L**ingering onward dreamily
> **I**n an evening of July—
> **C**hildren three that nestle near,
> **E**ager eye and willing ear,
> **P**leased a simple tale to hear—
>
> **L**ong has paled that sunny sky:
> **E**choes fade and memories die:
> **A**utumn frosts have slain July.
>
> **S**till she haunts me, phantomwise,
> **A**lice moving under skies

Never seen by waking eyes.

Children yet, the tale to hear,
Eager eye and willing ear,
Lovingly shall nestle near.

In a Wonderland they lie,
Dreaming as the days go by,
Dreaming as the summers die:

Ever drifting down the stream—
Lingering in the golden gleam—
Life, what is it but a dream?

Anyone can come up with acrostics. Here's one I just made up for the word 'BIRTHDAY'. As you can see, it is very simple, and doesn't have to rhyme.

Balloons fly about
In the evening sky
Right to the top
To ask far as the eye can see
Hungry children mill about
Darting from one end to the other
Awaiting the promised cake
'Yay!' they shouted, when it was brought out.

(a) Why don't you try to make one for the same word?

BIRTHDAY

_____
_____
_____
_____
_____

(b) Now, why don't you try making acrostics for these words:

 i) JUPITER
 ii) UNANIMOUS

5. **Acronyms**, on the other hand, are abbreviations from the *initial letters* of words, and can sometimes be pronounced as a word (see Chapter 3). Some examples are 3D (three dimensional), LPG (liquefied petroleum gas), OTP (one-time password), and so on. Acronyms help shorten long, and sometimes complicated, chains of texts. Acronyms are also useful while studying, as we saw with the examples of the colours of the rainbow, and the order of planets.

Sometimes, people take actual words and **expand** them as if they were acronyms. This can be quite a lot of fun and can help you learn the spellings of some new or hard words.

Here's an example for the name Meghna:

Most **E**lephants **G**o **H**ome, **N**ever **A**way

Sounds strange, doesn't it?

(a) Imagine your name is actually an acronym. Using the letters of your name, make **two** different expanded acronyms, like the one above.

(b) Try making similar words for:

 i) A morning routine: Brush Floss Bathe Dress Eat Pack Leave

ii) The words: SCANDAL HARBOUR

(Refer to Chapter 3 for more examples)

(c) How many common acronyms can you think of?

Worksheet 5

1. For one week, keep a notebook of new words and phrases that you come across. This may be in English, your mother tongue, or any language that you may be learning. Note down the meaning(s) and synonyms (if any), and write down two sentences using that word.

Alternatively, look up two new words a day in a dictionary and write them down in your notebook, with meaning and example.

If you recall, *how* you write it is as important as the act of writing. Using **different fonts, sizes and colours** will make the information stand out.

Here are some English words to get you started:
Effulgent Jejune Parvenu Disject Comportment

If you do not have your notebook with you, use any of the memory techniques in the book to remember the word till you get to a pen or pencil and can write it down.

If you continue doing this, you will build up your own **personal dictionary** of all the words that you have learnt. It is a great way to track your growth in a particular language. If you get one of your friends to join you, you can exchange words, or even use them in conversation. The best way to remember is to keep using it.

2. Is there any language you are currently learning? If so,

walk around the room you are in and see how many objects you can name in that language—things on the floor, furniture, linen, etc.

3. In keeping with the earlier exercise, look at the below picture. It is a reproduction of a famous painting 'Bedroom in Arles' by Vincent Van Gogh.

Source: Wikimedia Commons/V. Van Gogh

Can you name all the objects in it in languages **other than English**?

_____

_____

_____

Now, in your **first language**, write or orally provide as detailed a description of this room as you can. Describe the position of all the objects. What do you think the inhabitant of the room was like? Neat? Messy? Did they like the room? What do you like or dislike about the place?

4. Story prompt: We have started a story below. Either orally or through writing, or even through images with captions or speech bubbles, take the story forward! Think of how the story can proceed and put it down.

It was a hot, sunny day in the middle of the city, right along the river. In front of a little tea-stall at the water's edge two men sat staring into the water. They had been sitting there for half an hour and hadn't even looked at each other. The road was deserted—who would step out in this heat?

Even the men seemed to have fallen asleep in their chairs. All of a sudden, one of the chairs tilted too far and the man went toppling right over into the river! The other man looked up, startled...

5. Have you heard of **fanfiction**? It is a genre in which fans write stories about characters from the books or TV series they really enjoyed, for fun. For example, there are many websites where *Harry Potter* fans have written scenes from Harry's home when he was a baby or what happened after they all grew older and had children of their own. These are new stories fans imagine, based on minute details in the books.

Recall a book, TV show or movie you really enjoyed and, either by yourself or with your friends, develop new stories based on the characters and actual incidents that happened in the original. This way, you are recalling and fixing important or even trivial information in your mind *and* using language in a novel way, so you can revise words you know or exercise your creative skills! If you are working with someone else, this also gives you a chance to exchange ideas and learn new words from each other.

Perhaps you could try **roleplaying** this story you have come up with. After all, it is your story—you should be able decide to which character you are, and what he or she is like!

Answer Key

The answers given here are for the worksheets and exercises found in this book. Please note that some of the questions ask for *your* opinion or experience, or are specific to whichever language that *you* are learning or working with, and therefore, there cannot be one single correct answer.

Chapter 1: Memory: How It Works

1. a - ii b - iii c - i
2. a) True b) False

Chapter 4: Speaking and Listening

Worksheet 1

1. (c) No, it does not! It takes on the 'z' sound.
2. (a) i) lips, Y, N, N ii) tongue/roof of mouth, N, Y, N iii) lips, N, N, N iv) lips, N N, Y/N v) teeth/tongue, N, Y, Y vi) tongue/roof of mouth, N, N, Y vii) tongue/roof of mouth, N, Y, N vii) back of mouth, N, N, N

Chapter 6: Techniques for Revision and Further Practice

(a) i) 'baggy grey shepherd's check trousers, a not over-clean black frock-coat, unbuttoned in the front, and a drab waistcoat with a heavy brassy Albert chain, and a square pierced bit of metal dangling down as an ornament', 'a frayed top-hat and a faded brown overcoat with a

wrinkled velvet collar'.
ii) The muscles in his right hand were larger and more developed than his left.
iii) Watson thought him as an average British tradesman—'obese, pompous, and slow'.
iv) That he has done considerable amount of writing recently.

Final Worksheets

Worksheet 1

2. (a) i) гот ii) трембл iii) драстик
   (c) i, ii
7. (a) i) 'Carrot', referring to her red hair.
   ii) She gets angry and hits him on the head with her slate.

Worksheet 3

2. (a) i) Бук ii) Юниконз (or Юникорнз) iii) Прокрастинет
   iv) Коншинс

Worksheet 4

1. Pronunciations in English:
   kali-MEH-ra, ei-kha-ris-THO, si-GNO-mi, vo-EE-thee-ia, para-ka-LO

Bibliography

Angier, Natalie, 'Deaf Babies Use Their Hands To Babble, Researcher Finds', *The New York Times*, 22 March 1991. Available at https://www.nytimes.com/1991/03/22/us/deaf-babies-use-their-hands-to-babble-researcher-finds.html (accessed in 2018)

Atkinson, R.C. and Shiffrin, R.M., 'Human Memory: A Proposed System and its Control Processes,' In K.W. Spence and J.T. Spence (eds.), *The Psychology of Learning and Motivation: Advances in research and theory*, Vol. 2, pp. 89–195, Academic Press, New York, 1968.

Chemin, A., 'Handwriting vs Typing: Is the Pen Still Mightier than the Keyboard?' 2014. Available at https://www.theguardian.com/science/2014/dec/16/cognitive-benefits-handwriting-decline-typing (accessed in 2018)

Clemens, Z., Fabó, D. and Halász, P., 'Overnight Verbal Memory Retention Correlates with the Number of Sleep Spindles', *Neuroscience*, 132(2): 529–35, 2005. Available at https://doi.org/10.1016/J.NEUROSCIENCE.2005.01.011 (accessed in 2018)

Craik, F.I.M. and Lockhart, R.S., 'Levels of Processing: A Framework for Memory Research', *Journal of Verbal Learning and Verbal Behavior*, 11(6): 671–84, 1972.

Delistraty, C.C., 'For a Better Brain, Learn Another Language', 2014. Available at https://www.theatlantic.com/health/archive/2014/10/more-languages-better-brain/381193/ (accessed in 2018)

Eichenbaum, H. (ed.), *The Cognitive Neuroscience of Memory: An Introduction*, Oxford University Press, 2002.

Evans, V., *The Language Myth: Why Language is Not an Instinct*, Cambridge University Press, Cambridge, 2014.

Fromkin, V.A., Rodman, R.D. and Hyams, N.M., *An Introduction to Language*. S. l.: Wadsworth Cengage Learning, Boston, USA, 2013.

Gluck, M., Mercado, Eduardo and Myers, Catherine E., *Learning and Memory: From Brain to Behavior* (Third ed.), Worth Publishers, Macmillan Learning, New York, 2016.

Grant, A., 'How Memory Research Can Help You Learn a New Language', 2016. Available at https://aeon.co/ideas/how-memory-research-can-help-you-learn-a-new-language (accessed in 2018)

Joëls, M., Pu, Z., Wiegert, O., Oitzl, M.S. and Krugers, H.J., 'Learning under Stress: How Does it Work?' *Trends in Cognitive Sciences*, 10(4): 152–58, 2006. Available at https://doi.org/10.1016/J.TICS.2006.02.002 (accessed in 2018)

Kolb, B. and Whishaw, I.Q., *Fundamentals of Human Neuropsychology*, Worth Publishers, New York, 2015.

Merritt, A., 'Why Learn a Foreign Language? Benefits of Bilingualism', 2013. Available at https://www.telegraph.co.uk/education/educationopinion/10126883/Why-learn-a-foreign-language-Benefits-of-bilingualism.html (accessed in 2018)

Stanford Encyclopedia of Philosophy. Available at https://plato.stanford.edu/entries/innateness-language/ (accessed in 2018)

Sternberg, R.J. and Sternberg, K., *Cognitive Psychology, Seventh edition*. Wadsworth Publishing, 2016.

Stickgold, R., 'Sleep-dependent Memory Consolidation,' *Nature*, 437(7063): 1272–78, 2005.

The Conversation, 'Sign Languages are Fully-fledged, Natural Languages with their Own Dialects–they need protecting', 2019. Available at https://theconversation.com/sign-languages-are-fully-fledged-natural-languages-with-their-own-dialects-they-need-protecting-109388 (accessed in 2019)

Thurston, C.M., *Survival Tips for New Teachers: From People Who Have Been There, and Lived to Tell About It*, Cottonwood Press, Fort Collins, CO, 2009.

Wixted, J.T., 'The Psychology and Neuroscience of Forgetting', *Annual Review of Psychology*, 55(1): 235–69, 2004. Available at https://

doi.org/10.1146/annurev.psych.55.090902.141555 (accessed in 2018)

Wolf, O.T., 'Stress and Memory in Humans: Twelve Years of Progress?' *Brain Research*, 1293: 142–54, 2009.

Wright, A., Betteridge, D. and Buckby, M., *Games for Language Learning*, Cambridge University Press, Cambridge, 2012.

Wyner, G., *Fluent Forever: How to Learn any Language* Fast *and Never Forget It*, Harmony Books, New York, 2014.

Acknowledgements

The authors would like to thank Rupa Publications, Delhi, and Yamini Chowdhury and Priya Talwar, our editors, for giving us the opportunity to work on this book.

Akhila would like to thank her Besant Arundale Senior Secondary School B.A.S.S. (Kalakshetra) librarian and teachers who encouraged lateral thinking and wide reading; her Psychology professors at Women's Christian College (WCC), Chennai; her parents, whose multilingualism has helped her own exploration of languages and who helped read through the book; and finally, her partner Berty, thanks to whom this project came about and got completed.

Meghna would like to thank her professors from Ambedkar University Delhi, who opened her eyes to the world around her, and in particular, her Linguistics professor, who ignited an interest that hasn't (yet!) burned out. She would also like to thank her friends and family, who have helped her through tough times, and lastly, her father—her companion and anchor.